THE COUNSEL
OF A FRIEND

12 Ways to Put Your
Caring Heart into Action

THE COUNSEL OF A FRIEND

12 Ways to Put Your Caring Heart into Action

Lynda D. Elliott

Thomas Nelson Publishers
Nashville

Published in Nashville, Tennessee, by Janet Thoma Books, a division of
Thomas Nelson, Inc., Publishers, and distributed in Canada by Word
Communications, Ltd., Richmond, British Columbia, and in the
United Kingdom by Word (UK), Ltd., Milton Keynes, England.

Printed in the United States of America

98 97 96 95 94 93   8 7 6 5 4 3 2 1

Unless otherwise noted, all Scripture quotations are from The Amplified Bible, Old Testament, copyright 1962, 1964, by the Zondervan
Publishing House, or The Amplified Bible, New Testament, copyright
1958, by The Lockman Foundation.

Library of Congress Cataloging-in-Publication Data

Elliot, Lynda D.
    Counsel of a friend / by Lynda D. Elliot.
      p. cm.
    ISBN 0-8407-7826-0
    1. Peer counseling in the church. 2. Friendship—Religious
aspects—Christianity. 3. Counseling. I. Title.
BV4409.E54 1993
253.5—dc20
                                       93–10281
                                         CIP

To

David, Wayne, Brenda,
Kristina,
Sam and Susan,

with love

CONTENTS

ACKNOWLEDGMENTS

I would like to thank my agents Wolgemuth & Hyatt for confirming God's will to me in the writing of *The Counsel of a Friend*. Your encouragement, friendship, and support mean much to me.

I am especially grateful to Karen D'Arezzo for the hours spent editing the first draft! Your wise suggestions and expertise enabled me to write with clarity. You were constantly there with the encouragement that kept me going. Thank you for your efforts, your love, and your counsel!

To the men and women I have seen in individual and group counseling, I offer my gratitude. I have learned much from seeing God work in your lives, and I pray that, as you read this book, you will rejoice in seeing your struggles transformed into help for others.

I appreciate so much my faithful friends who consistently prayed for me from the beginning of this book: Carolyn Johnson, Betty O'Neal, Kittie Hoofman, Janis Shull, Fran Fought, and Beckie Sudduth. Your prayers, love, and faithfulness sustained me.

Above all, I thank God for guiding me in the writing of this book. I offer it to Him, for His glory and for help to His people.

THE COUNSEL OF A FRIEND

Oil and perfume rejoice the heart; so does the sweetness
of a friend's counsel that comes from the heart.
PROVERBS 27:9

Jesus kept me alive through my friends!" said Janet, a pretty, vibrant, dark-haired woman, the speaker at my monthly prayer luncheon. As she stood before us, it was difficult to imagine her being anything other than full of life!

"On a Sunday morning two years ago," she continued, "my husband came home from church, sat down in his recliner, and said, 'I want out.' We had been married for twenty-eight years and had three children. I never dreamed this would happen to our family. I had married for life, and I thought we adored each other!

"I cannot tell you how much I loved that man! In spite of what he said that day, he was not a mean man. He was a wonderful husband and a wonderful father. What happened? I still don't know, but within thirty days, we were divorced. Two weeks later, he remarried. Our lifestyle changed completely. Even with child support, our income was cut by more than half.

"For a year I was in shock. I hadn't seen this coming. My children hadn't seen it coming. It was as if we had all been run over by a truck. It didn't just affect me—it happened to all of us—the children, my mother-in-law, our friends, and my brothers and sisters. We were all grief-stricken!

"Soon after my husband left, my thirteen-year-old daughter tried to harm herself. Afterward, she asked me, 'Mama, why did Daddy leave us?' I put her in my bed and we cried all night.

"Sometimes in the mornings, I would awaken to the sound of a woman in my bedroom screaming and sobbing. I would realize that the sound was coming from my own throat. My grief almost overwhelmed me.

"I don't know what I would have done without my four friends. They placed a blanket of love over me during that first year of shock. They were my life-support system! The day after word got out that my husband had left, they sent me a beautiful bouquet of spring flowers with a card saying, 'We are here if you need us.' Weeks later, when I felt like going out, they invited me for pizza. In their company, I felt like someone who had just come in out of the cold on a winter night. They took me out every Friday night for a year and helped me feel like somebody again.

"Their prayers, caring, and Spirit-led counsel sustained my family and me during those dark months. When I was feeling down, a note with a Scripture verse or a prayer would arrive at just the right time. It was amazing how a little note in the mail could carry me for days.

"When my daughter could not afford a school annual, I received a note with money for it. When I would wear a dress to church too many times, my friends came over with a new dress. They helped me with Christmas that first year. Because of those friends, we actually had a marvelous Christmas!

"No matter what the need or the situation, God provided exactly what I and my family needed through my friends. I couldn't have made it without them!"

The counsel, encouragement, and love of a friend *can* make the difference in the life of someone who is struggling with problems. You may feel that you need specialized training in order to be an effective helper or that you need to have all areas of your own life in order before you can help. Knowledge is important, and in each of the following chapters, you will gain some information that you may not already have. But more important than knowledge is a sincere desire to be used of God in the lives of others.

"It was amazing how a little note in the mail could carry me for days."

We have all been given the "ministry of reconciliation" (2 Corinthians 5:18). *The Counsel of a Friend* has been written to help you, as a "minister of reconciliation," become better equipped to be a helpful friend and counselor to those whom God puts in your life.

The Counsel of a Friend is divided into three sections.

The first section, "The Willing Heart," provides important information you will need *before* you begin working with a friend. You will want to refer to these chapters as you counsel, but you can save yourself much trial-and-error learning if you study these chapters before you get started.

The second section, "The Helping Heart," concerns specific problem areas. These can be read in any order, or some not at all, depending on the needs of your friend.

The third section, "The Steadfast Heart," should also be read *before*, as well as *during*, your work with your friend. In this section, ways are discussed to persevere through the problems of your friend and how to do spiritual battle, as well as ways to celebrate steps of progress with your friend.

At the end of each chapter are questions for small group discussion. You may use these questions to train people to work with others, or as aids to help you in applying the material in the chapters. The purposes of the questions include enabling individuals to identify both with the counselor "role" and the person in need, to identify personal strengths and weaknesses in the counseling relationship, to become comfortable expressing personal feelings and experiences, and to test the amount of knowledge gained from the chapter.

I am excited that you are interested in counseling others! Some of the most meaningful counsel I've observed has come *from the caring heart of a friend*. I pray that you, as well as those you counsel, will be blessed by our Father as you give others that same "comfort, consolation, and encouragement" (2 Corinthians 1:4) He has given to you.

"The divorce changed my life forever. It changed the lives of my children forever. But God healed me and my family. He placed us in His emergency room, and He sent us friends to be His physicians and nurses.

"Now I'm at a place where I can see the sun coming up in the mornings without a feeling of dread, where the grass is greener than it has ever been, where the landing of a single redbird causes my heart to swell with joy! I was brought to this place by Jesus, through my friends."

THE COUNSEL OF A FRIEND

12 Ways to Put Your Caring Heart into Action

——————————————————————— *PART ONE*

THE WILLING HEART

1

BUT I DON'T KNOW WHAT TO SAY!

> And Moses said to the Lord, O Lord, I am not
> eloquent or a man of words, neither before or
> since You have spoken to Your servant; for I am
> slow of speech and have a heavy and awkward
> tongue. And the Lord said to him, Who has made
> man's mouth? Or who makes the dumb, or the
> deaf, or the seeing, or the blind? Is it not I, the
> Lord? Now therefore go, and I will be with your
> mouth and will teach you what you shall say.
>
> EXODUS 4:10–12

I'd really like to help people," the pretty, redheaded woman told me, "but I'm afraid! There are so many people with problems. Problems I've never experienced. I don't have any training, and I wouldn't know what to say or to do! What if I tell someone the wrong thing? What if I cause someone to feel *worse* after I've 'counseled' them?"

You may be thinking these same things: "What if I don't know what to say? What if I say or do the wrong thing? How can I help someone if I haven't had the same problem? What if I don't have an answer?"

How did Janet's friends know what to say? How did they know what to do? How were they able to be her "life-support" system?

The Essential Ingredients

Janet knew her friends loved her. Someone once said, "People don't care what you know until they know you care." *The most important ingredient in the helping relationship is love.*

You can have all the knowledge in the world, but if your friend doesn't know that you care about her, you won't be helpful. In her crisis, Janet knew that she had friends loving her and standing by her. If a person feels she is cared about, she will get better. Love is a powerful force!

However, some people are easier to love than others. What if you don't *feel* love for the person you are trying to help?

One of my good friends, Beckie, told me of her struggle as she tried to *feel* love. Her dad deserted the family when she was young, and he was now sick and in need of a kidney transplant. She said to us, "My dad contacted me and told me of his illness. I told him I would give him one of my kidneys if he needed it. But I feel so bad because I just don't have any feelings for him and it seems that I should. Maybe, after all these years, I don't even love him."

Although we all enjoy warm feelings that can accompany love, love is not *just* a feeling. Love is a commitment.

Love is a choice. Beckie had made the commitment to love her dad. She had chosen to give him what she could of herself. You don't have to *feel* anything to love. Make the commitment and the choice to love.

Whether you feel love or not, to love in your own strength is impossible. God will give you the ability. He will pour His love into you and make you able. Feelings may or may not follow.

Never underestimate the strengthening power of God's love coming through you. Love provides the motivation for you to persevere, and love takes away your friend's hollow feeling of aloneness.

"Moses didn't have to have great speaking abilities in order for God to use him."

Love alone is not enough, however. Janet's friends did not merely love her; they put their love into tangible, helpful actions. Their availability and willingness to offer spiritual help, money, companionship, and practical services made the difference.

A woman new to my community told me, "Several months before we moved, our oldest child died. I visited your church last Sunday, and I was so touched. When the woman sitting next to me learned of my situation, she offered to go with me to a group for bereaved parents. When she offered to do this, I knew she really wanted to help. Her willingness to help someone she didn't even know meant so much to me!"

But I Don't Know What to Say!

When Moses said to the Lord, "O Lord, I am not eloquent or a man of words, neither before nor since You have spoken to Your servant; for I am slow of speech and have a heavy and awkward tongue" (Exodus 4:10), God didn't require him to take a speech class before He used him. Instead, God said to him, "Who has made man's mouth? Or who makes the dumb, or the deaf, or the seeing, or the blind? Is it not I, the Lord? Now therefore go, and I will be with your mouth and will teach you what you shall say" (Exodus 4:11–12).

Moses didn't have to have great speaking abilities in order for God to use him. He didn't have to know what to say. God promised that He would teach him.

As you work with your friend, you don't have to know all the jargon, have a Scripture verse for each problem ready on the tip of your tongue, or be an effective communicator. There are some things, however, that will help to equip you.

Study God's Word

Bill told me, "My wife has always attended Bible studies and memorized Scripture, but I had never been at all interested until one night when I got up to comfort our young son who was having a nightmare. As I lay down beside him, I said, 'It's okay, son. You don't need to be afraid. Daddy's here.' His sobbing and trembling continued as I attempted to hold him. Suddenly, this four-year-old boy remembered something and exclaimed, 'What time I am afraid, I will trust in God' (Psalm 56:3). He immediately became still in my arms, and fell asleep.

"I realized that this was the verse he had been studying in Sunday school. I saw firsthand the power of the Word.

Since that time, I have studied the Scripture and applied His Word to my own life. Now, when I try to help a friend, I have many Scripture verses that God has made real in my own life. I feel like these personal stories have made more of an impact on my friends than anything else I have said."

Spend time daily studying the Word and apply it consistently in your own problems. If you are going to be comfortable using God's Word to help others, you must know through your own experience that His Word speaks to you directly. Many sources are available to help you, including concordances, study Bibles, topical Bibles, promise books, and commentaries. Take the time to study His Word.

Second Timothy 2:15 states: "Study and be eager and do your utmost to present yourself to God approved (tested by trial), a workman who has no cause to be ashamed, correctly analyzing and accurately dividing [rightly handling and skillfully teaching] the Word of Truth." As you study the Word of God, His Spirit will teach you the truth, and the truth that you learn will set others free (John 8:32).

Use God's Word

When you don't know what to say, let God's Word speak for you! To avoid sounding like one who "knows it all," you might say, "I'm not sure what I think about that. Let's see what God's Word says about it."

Hebrews 4:12 says "For the Word that God speaks is alive and full of power. . . ." When you speak God's Word to your friend, the power within it will do its work. God's Word will accomplish His purpose and will always produce effects (Isaiah 55:11), whether these are visible to you or not.

God's Word is the most powerful persuader that exists. His thoughts are absolutely correct, and He implants the power within them to enable your friend to respond if she chooses.

It is important, however, to use wisdom. Jack told me, "I really like Dick, but whenever I tell him about a problem I'm having, he starts quoting verses to me. I know God's Word will help me, but I just wish Dick would share a little bit of himself, instead of preaching to me."

As you share what God says with your friend, share yourself. Let her know how God is using His Word in your life. Be aware of the difference between sharing Scripture verses *with* your friend and quoting Scripture verses *at* her.

Pray

When you don't know what to say, ask God! God is the only One who knows what your friend needs to hear, so as you talk with your friend, stay tuned in to God through prayer. It is easy to get God's ear, and you can be confident of His concern.

Let your friend know you are praying for her. Pray as specifically as you are able for her needs, as well as your own. As you and she share the answers to your prayers, faith will grow.

Who Am I to Help Anyone?

"How can I help anyone else? Look at what a mess I've made of my own life! I don't know enough. How can I even offer to help?"

You may feel that you can't help anyone else because of your own past sins and mistakes. If only people who had lived perfect lives could qualify as counselors, *no one* could ever help another person! No one except Jesus has lived without sins or mistakes. We all have a "past," but if you have given your life to Jesus, He will take what you have learned from past sins and mistakes and show you how to use it to help others. Even if you are a brand-new Christian, you have the knowledge and personal experience of salvation that a lost friend needs. You have much to give!

William, a man in his mid-thirties, was very successful in the business world. After his conversion, he began discipling other men. When I met him, he was leading several prayer groups for men, had written a book on how to know God, and continued to be successful in business. He told me, "I think the reason other men will listen to me is that they know I have many of the same temptations and problems they face. At first, I thought I had to have all the answers. But I found that sharing what God has done for me and where I am in my present struggles really helps other men!"

When you are tempted to feel unworthy to help, remember that there is no more condemnation for you (Romans 8:1). You are as white as snow! If you have confessed your sins, you couldn't be any cleaner! Jesus has chosen you and made you worthy to serve Him and others. As He told His disciples: "You have not chosen Me, but I have chosen you" (John 15:16).

God's hand of approval is extended to you. Put your hand in His, and by His Spirit begin to offer yourself to Him.

Is It All Right to Admit "I Don't Know"?

You don't need to have the answer to every question. In fact, sometimes you won't have any idea of the answer or a solution. It is completely acceptable to say "I don't know. Why don't we pray together for an answer?" or "I don't know. Let's both try to get some more information." Your friend needs to be fully aware that you do not have all the answers.

When wisdom is needed, refer to James 1:5: "If any of you is deficient in wisdom, let him ask of the giving God [Who gives] to everyone liberally and ungrudgingly, without reproaching or faultfinding, and it will be given him."

By saying, "I don't know," you will have another opportunity to point your friend directly to Jesus and provide another chance to learn from His Word.

If I Haven't Had the Same Problem, Can I Help?

It is not necessary to have had the same experience as your friend. Sometimes when we have had the same problem, we tend to overidentify and our judgment can become clouded. You may never be in the same situations or experience the identical problems, but you can identify with your friend's feelings and you can acquire knowledge that you may need.

Robert was a single man in his late twenties, but his friend had been married for ten years. The friend and his wife were having problems, and he asked Robert, "If you've never been married, how can you help me?"

Robert replied, "Although I've not been married, I have felt the same way you're feeling, so I understand. I learned a lot through some of the problems I've had in relationships. I think I might be of help."

Never underestimate the value of your presence. Jeanne told me of an experience in which she didn't know what to say or do: "I visited my aunt in the hospital when her child was critically ill. I felt terrible because, on one particular day, I was extremely tired, and I didn't feel that I was able to do or say anything helpful." Later she found that her aunt had not even noticed that she had been tired because she had been so absorbed by concern for her son. Her aunt told her that it had been such a comfort just to have someone in the room with her so that she was not alone.

Jesus realized the value of "presence" when He said, "I will not leave you as orphans [comfortless, desolate, bereaved, forlorn, helpless]; I will come [back] to you" (John 14:18). Don't feel that you always have to "do something" or "say something" important for your presence to be helpful.

Your presence, your empathy, your love, and your prayers can make a great difference.

How Will I Know What to Do?

"Even though I know God has chosen me, I still feel so inadequate. What if I do the wrong thing?"

Inadequacy is good! Realizing that you *are* inadequate is actually spiritual maturity.

Knowing that you *don't* know what to do, and that you must have the constant guidance from God's Word and the Holy Spirit, is necessary before you can be effectively used by God.

"Never underestimate the value of your presence."

Paul reminded the early Christians: "Not that we are fit [qualified and sufficient in ability] of ourselves . . ." (2 Corinthians 3:5). Rest assured that God will work in you to make you able. Throughout the Scriptures, oil poured out on people symbolized God's anointing. At Pentecost,

11

however, the Holy Spirit Himself was poured out upon all believers, and God came to empower them. Pray to be filled with the Holy Spirit, and you will have His ability.

Living in Him

Consider this: "For in Him we live and move and have our being" (Acts 17:28). As you work with your friend, remember that you are "in Him." God will make you able as you dwell in Him.

Several years ago, I had a remarkable experience with God. I had begun to spend several hours each day in Bible study and prayer. One morning as I was sitting in the bedroom, I sensed a presence enter the room. The power that came from that presence was so great that I can only call it "overshadowing." It was as if He were waiting. I had never experienced such a revelation of power before, and I was afraid. I knew that if I invited that presence to touch me in any way, I would never be the same again.

Thoughts of caution came to my mind. What if it wasn't God? I knew that I wanted no other power than the Holy Spirit to touch me. I prayed, "Father, if that *is* You, please confirm Yourself to me."

The presence did not seem to move, and so I went about my day, ever aware that He was there. I felt almost as if I were in a dream, but I was able to carry out my responsibilities without any hindrances.

The presence continued with me for several days, and the next Sunday in church when we were singing a praise song, tears began to run down my face. The presence continued to overshadow me, although there was still no direct confirmation.

A few days later, I was driving home and having become almost accustomed to the presence, I prayed, "Father, if that is truly Your Spirit, I want You to do whatever You have come to do." Nothing happened for several days. In fact, it seemed as if the presence withdrew to some extent.

One morning later that week, as I was driving to a nearby town, I rounded a curve and drove down into a valley lined by large oak trees. As the sun shone down through the early morning mist, the presence was suddenly with me again. Inside myself I heard Him speak to me and say, "I am God, the Father of Christ Jesus." He had confirmed His identity to me!

As I drove, He continued to speak to me. He said, "Before, I came into you. It is time now for you to come into Me." I pulled over and wrote down all that had been said to me.

This was not a particularly intense, emotional experience, but it was a very profound one that I shall never forget. From that moment, His words began a great change inside of me.

When I got home, I began to read the many verses in Ephesians and Colossians that began with "In Him. . . ." I began to understand what He had wanted me to know: when I was saved, Jesus had come to me in my need. I had needed Him to help me, and for a long time, our relationship was centered around *His* meeting *my* needs. I had received help and healing in many areas. But now it was time for me to stop focusing on my own needs and to allow Him to begin using me more to help meet the needs of others.

At that point, He taught me more about His purposes for His people—not just His purposes for me—and with His words came the desire to serve and a new power of anointing, so that I could be used by Him in new ways.

It is an honor and a joy to be chosen to live beyond the boundaries of our own lives and problems. It is an adventure to learn to do what Jesus did!

LIFE APPLICATIONS ————————————

1. Have you ever felt completely alone? What did you need that you did not have?

2. Have you ever held back because you were afraid you wouldn't have an immediate answer?

3. Has anyone ever "preached" at you or become exasperated and simply read you a Scripture out of frustration? How did you feel?

4. Do you find yourself struggling to think of answers rather than praying and waiting for answers to be given by God?

5. Have you ever felt disqualified to help because of past sins, mistakes, or failures? Can you give an example?

6. Has anyone ever said to you, "But you can't know how I feel, because it hasn't happened to you"? What did you do?

7. Can you remember a time when someone's presence was a comfort to you? Can you share that experience?

8. What is the "worst thing" anyone has ever done in an attempt to help you?

9. Can you think of a time when you could not have made it without the help of another person? Who was that person? How did he or she help you? Was he or she an "expert?"

2

WON'T SOMEONE LISTEN TO ME?

Blessed is the man who listens. . . .
PROVERBS 8:34

*H*ave you ever talked with someone who wouldn't let you finish your sentences? Or who talked constantly and never gave you a chance to say anything? Or who looked around the room while you were talking? Or yawned? Or even worse, fell asleep?

All of us have had experiences like this, and we probably have acquired some bad listening habits ourselves. Listening may appear easy or even passive, but really "hearing" another person may be the hardest work you will do. Yet among the most important gifts you can give a friend is a listening ear. It is rare to find a good listener. No wonder that Solomon said, "Blessed is the man who listens . . ." (Proverbs 8:34).

Do you listen? Sometimes others give us the real truth about our listening skills. Has anyone ever said to you,

"But Mom, I tried to tell you!" or

"Stop interrupting me!" or

"I've answered that question twice already!" or

"Will you *please* let me *finish?*"

If you have a hard time listening, don't give up. By practicing some specific listening skills and asking God to give you ears that hear, you can be a person who hears even beyond the words that are spoken.

Foundations of Listening

Who are the people to whom you reveal personal matters? Many times when our souls long to reach out to talk to someone, we remain silent. Why are we silent at those times when we have an overwhelming need to be heard? Perhaps it may be because we have often found others to be untrustworthy.

One woman admitted that although she had always wanted to have a "best friend," she had never really been able to fully trust anyone. She related her story, filled with lost hopes and misplaced trust.

> I was my mother's youngest child. For some reason I didn't resemble any of the other family members. I remember remarks made by relatives that gave me the idea that my father wasn't really my real dad. My older sister was the favorite. Everybody noticed her, not me. I always kept to myself and covered my feelings, because I didn't know what else to do. They thought I had it all together, however.
>
> One day when I was about four, Mother suddenly left my sister and me and ran off with another man. My dad

remarried, but my stepmother didn't want me. I was mostly raised by grandparents who were kind, but who didn't really understand me. I felt unwanted, unloved, and different all my life.

I married a man who abused me and our little son. By the time we divorced, I felt totally unlovable. Then I married my present husband. He really cares about me, but I have been afraid to fully give myself to him. I have been afraid that someday he, too, will leave me.

I've made efforts to confide in friends, but they interpreted my façade as calm composure and didn't recognize my needs. It's hard for me to express myself. I desperately want friends, but I am ashamed of my past and afraid of rejection and betrayal. Would anyone really care enough to listen?

Before she could become vulnerable, she had to learn to trust. And that is how it is with all of us. All of us have been hurt in at least one area of our lives. Many hide those wounds for years because of the fear of further rejection from others. How can we help others to trust us? How do we communicate that we want to listen, and then how do we really hear them?

"Many times when our souls long to reach out to talk to someone, we remain silent. Why? . . . Perhaps it may be because we have often found others to be untrustworthy."

Be Trustworthy

Can you keep a confidence? Or do you need to feel impor-tant by letting others know that *you* know things they aren't privy to? It may be very tempting to discuss things you hear in confidence, especially if it involves well-known people.

One of the most "innocent," but doubly deadly, ways we can break a confidence is in the name of the Lord. We can spiritualize our betrayal! Have you ever been at a prayer meeting and heard someone pray, "Father, please help the Smiths work out their marriage problems"? Without his saying anything specific, in the name of praying for a fel-low Christian, this betrayal may have created more suspi-cion and caused more harm than if all the details of the Smiths' problems had been discussed openly.

When you feel tempted to betray a confidence, question your motive. Would you freely discuss this in front of the person concerned? Would you want to be overheard? Will telling these "facts" further the kingdom of Christ? Is your motive to be accepted or look important? Are you spiritual-izing your need to show off how "concerned" you are?

Share Yourself

It is much easier to talk to a person who doesn't pretend to be perfect!

A friend told me of a church retreat she had attended in which the participants were asked to share where they had been and where they were going. One woman, in particu-lar, impressed me with her willingness to share about her multiple marriages, the sins she had committed, and the grace God had shown her, as well as her current struggles with her now-grown children. She didn't glamorize the sins, as do many who give testimonies; nor did she paint a rosy picture of her victories. But her words were surrounded by the power of Jesus in her life and His mercy, grace, and strength. She didn't pretend to be superspiritual, yet there was a refreshing spirituality and innocence about her. She was real, and Jesus was magnified.

Since that time, when I think of people I would trust to talk with on a deep level, I have thought of her. She was free to be herself and to share what Jesus was doing in her life.

Identify with the Feeling

Often, you may be unable to identify with a person's problem or situation. Your husband may never have left you; your sister may not be dying of cancer; your children may not be having trouble in school—but you can identify with the *feeling*.

Listen for the universal feeling. Is it anger? Guilt? Sadness? Frustration? Hopelessness?

If you can, tell your friend about a time when you have *felt* that same way. Let her know that you have heard the feelings behind the words she has said. However, in your enthusiasm to let your friend know you identify with her, don't go into your life story! She will probably be too concerned about her own feelings and situation to be that interested in yours at that point. Your sharing should simply be a way of communicating that you are hearing her—not a monologue about yourself! Remember, you are the listener!

Go Slowly

Confiding in another person may be a new experience for your friend, and it may take her some time to be able to express her thoughts. She may also be afraid of your rejection or disapproval and need to go slowly. Let her go at her own pace as she tells you her story.

19

People may have specific reasons for not wanting to give details immediately. For example, one woman who came to me for counseling didn't want me to file her insurance because her claims would reveal her maiden name. Her parents were leaders in the Christian community, and so she was sure I was acquainted with them. Years earlier, she had seen another counselor who attended the same church as her parents. After she poured out her heart to this counselor about the rejection and emotional abuse she had experienced growing up, he replied, "I find that hard to believe. Your parents are the So-and-So's. I can't believe they would have done those things to you!" At that point, she dropped out of counseling. Years later, when she finally sought help again, she vowed her next counselors would never know her parents' identities.

The Essential Ingredients

Listening is a skill that must be learned. As with any other skill, certain factors are important if we are to be successful.

Body Language

Her body language. "I really don't know why I'm here. When I first called you to make the appointment, I was feeling down. But now I feel okay. I almost didn't come," one young woman said, sitting with her hands clenched, shoulders bowed, eyes downcast, and voice low. Her words certainly didn't match the messages of her body.

When you listen to others, the words they say are only a small part of the message they are trying to convey. Look into the eyes of your friend. Are they clear and sparkling? Closed and aloof? Do you see hurt? Does she have trouble looking at you?

Look at her mouth. Is it tight and drawn? Does her smile reach to her eyes? Do you notice any nervous twitches in her facial muscles?

What about her hands? Are they tightly gripped or lying at ease in her lap? Is she fidgeting with a string on the chair, the hair on her arms, a paper in her hands?

Are her shoulders straight or slumped? Does your friend sit back comfortably in her chair, or does she sit on the edge, poised to leave at any moment? Does she get up and walk around, or does she change position frequently? Does she talk to you while gazing at a point over your head? Are her arms crossed or open? Does she seem very controlled and stiff? Does she appear embarrassed to cry or show emotion? Do you hear any emotion in her voice, or does she talk in a monotone?

The answers to these questions will provide you with as much information as her actual words will, especially in the beginning of your relationship.

Examine all of the clues a person gives you. What is she saying? What are the nonverbal messages? Sometimes these will be congruent and at other times they won't. Ask God to give you spiritual discernment so that you can see beyond the physical and hear beyond the words to the hurting heart inside.

Your body language. Your body, as well as your words, will also be giving your friend certain messages. While she is talking to you, are you waiting for a chance to express your opinion or to tell her what to do? Are you looking around the room to see what else is going on? Do you keep looking at your watch, or are you fidgeting in your chair? Do you find yourself wishing she would hurry up and get to the point?

Do you allow judgmental expressions to cross your face?

If a person sees the reflection of judgment within you, she will stop sharing honestly and fully. Is your expression one of caring and compassion or one of impatience and judgment?

Denying Yourself

Listening is a work which takes all of a person's mental, emotional, and sometimes even physical energies. Really hearing a person requires that you set aside your own thoughts, your own agenda, your own preconceived ideas, and concentrate totally on the thoughts of the other person. *In fact, true listening is an art of self-denial.*

How often have you had a telephone conversation with a friend while you were also doing the dishes or straightening your desk? This is not to say that casual conversation cannot be enjoyed under these circumstances, but when you do this, you are giving the person the message that what she is saying (even if it is not about something important) is not worthy of your complete attention. If she is offended by this, she will then be less likely to talk to you about what is really bothering her, and this may be the real reason she called.

Giving your full attention to another is an act of self-denial because you are putting her agenda ahead of your own.

Part of denying yourself while listening will be to practice learning to sense the pace of the other. You may believe you have an answer for her, but often it is wise to wait and ask God to show you if she is ready to hear the answer. If you run ahead of the other person with your solution, she will only feel forced into accepting your opinion, and she will resist your efforts to help. Remember, you can't move another person faster than she wants to go, no matter how clear the path may seem to you.

Don't Assume You Know What Is Needed

One Sunday afternoon a friend dropped in unexpectedly. She was visibly upset, lines of dried tears making streaks on her carefully made-up face. For the next hour, she poured out a story of marital distress. My heart went out to her as I listened. I so wanted to help. After she became calm, I gave her a few suggestions. As I began to elaborate, her attitude toward me cooled considerably. When I offered to pray with her, she suddenly stood up and announced she had to leave. When I asked what was wrong, she exclaimed, "I didn't come here for you to try to fix me! All I wanted was for you to listen!"

Don't assume you know what another person needs from you. It may not be what you think, and as a result, both of you may leave the encounter with hurt or misunderstood feelings. Ask, "Do you want my thoughts on this, or do you just need me to listen?"

This is particularly important in male-female relationships. When a male hears a problem, usually his first reaction is to fix it, to solve the problem. Many times, a woman just wants to be heard and understood. Unfortunately, the man doesn't know whether she needs a listening ear or a solution. Just ask if you aren't sure! And when you are the one who needs a listening ear, be sure to let your friend know. It will help you both!

Care Enough to Make Sure You Understand

Make comments, clarify, and ask questions about what you hear to make sure you understand. For example, when your friend tells you about her husband's hurtful words, you might reply, "You sound really upset about that. I know that really hurt." Or, "It sounds as if you were really disappointed. Now tell me again, when did that happen?" Caring enough to make sure you understand the situation lets her know you want to stand with her as a friend.

"Don't assume you know what another person needs from you. It may not be what you think."

Respect Feelings

Don't tell a person how she should feel! The fastest way to stop communication is to say, "You shouldn't say things like that!" or, "How could you feel that way?"

Many times we Christians don't share our doubts, negative feelings, or fears because we have been told by other well-meaning Christians, "You shouldn't feel like that. Why, you have Jesus!" We forget that Jesus had the same emotions we have. Having Jesus doesn't make us immune to sadness, heartaches, and doubts. Having Jesus makes us able to bear them because He feels them with us and He understands!

Be careful not to dictate another's feelings. This will cause a person to feel ashamed of her feelings and to cut herself off from your help, as well as the help of God Himself. There will be a time and place for you to impart counsel to her. At this point, however, your mission is primarily to listen.

Use the Word to Encourage

As you listen, ask God to bring to your mind His Word to apply to that situation. Ask for His guidance in using the

24

Word to talk to that person. This is very important, because sometimes Christians use the Word of God as a "fast fix" for people.

Howard was very leery about going to a Christian counselor because of past experiences with well-meaning, but perhaps overzealous Christians. His serious problem with anxiety, however, had begun to affect his work, his marriage, and his health. Acknowledging his problem, Howard finally confided in several Christian friends but concluded they caused him to feel even worse. "One of them told me it was a sin to worry and that I should repent! I already knew that. The reason I talked to him was to find out how *not* to worry! Another friend told me to trust God and get help from the Bible. I would, if I just knew how!" Howard felt that God was mad at him and that he was a failure. Instead of getting help from Scripture, he felt condemned by it.

As he faced his fears and learned ways to deal with them, Howard was able to see God's Word as a source of strength and encouragement to him. He needed someone to love him *with* the Word, not someone to try to give him a "fast fix."

The Divine Listener

What mental picture do you have when you think of God as a listener? Do you think of Him as listening only when you have something really important to say? Do you have to use certain words for God to hear you? Do you have to go through a formula of saying particular words before He will listen?

Many of our pictures of God the Father come from our experiences with our earthly fathers or caregivers. What kind of listening relationship did you have with your father? Did he take time to listen to you? Did he listen to the things that were unimportant as well as what was important? Could you count on him to really hear you?

Do's and Don'ts of Listening

Do:	Don't:
Try to maintain eye contact.	Look all around the room to see what else is going on.
Practice patience. Let the person tell her story in her own way.	Interrupt or finish a sentence for the other.
Keep your word.	Talk about what someone has told you in confidence.
Share yourself, but concentrate on listening.	Talk excessively about yourself.
Try to identify with the feeling.	Tell the person, "You shouldn't feel that way!"
Let the person know you feel honored to have been chosen to listen to her problem.	Pretend you have all the answers.
Let the person set her own pace.	Get mad when she isn't ready to do something you suggest.
Listen for both verbal and nonverbal messages.	Assume you have all the facts.
Be aware of your own body language and verbal messages.	Look horrified when you are told about the problem.
Try to give the other your full attention.	Try to write a term paper, study your Sunday school lesson, or prepare for a talk while you listen.
Ask questions.	Make hasty judgments.
Use the Word as you give of yourself.	Use the Word as a "fast fix."

As you counsel with others, you need to be assured that God will hear you, and that He will hear the people He has given you to help. And since there will be times when you are not available to listen to others, you need to direct them to Him. They need to know God as the Divine Listener. They need to know that God hears them.

When the person you are counseling feels discouraged, help her to remember the things God has provided and done in the past. One exercise that I have found to be extremely beneficial, using Psalm 107, is to write down all of the needs expressed that caused the people to cry out to the Lord and then to write down God's response. For example, they were hungry and without a home, and they cried to the Lord. He "delivered them out of their distresses. He led them forth by the straight and right way, that they might go to a city where they might establish their homes" (Psalm 107:6–7).

Will Someone Listen to Me?

Yes! Our Father will always be available to listen. Sometimes other people won't or can't listen—but God will always be there. He will hear not only our words but also our hearts. He will always take time for us, no matter who we are. He will listen to our problems and complaints. And He will run to our cries!

As you begin your work with others, always point them to the Divine Listener—the One Who loves, cares, listens, and rescues.

> There is none like God . . . Who rides through the heavens to your help and in His majestic glory through the skies. The eternal God is your refuge and dwelling place, and underneath are the everlasting arms. (Deuteronomy 33:26–27)

LIFE APPLICATIONS ————————————

1. Has anyone ever broken your confidence? How did you feel?

2. Have you ever broken anyone's confidence and then been caught? What did you do? In looking back, what could you have done to avoid that mistake?

3. Have you ever felt closer to someone after they shared a current struggle with you? How is this different from just hearing past victories?

4. What does your body do when you become angry or anxious?

5. When you get restless or let your attention wander, what do you do?

6. Have you ever assumed someone wanted your advice, only to find out later you have offended them by giving it? What happened?

7. Has anyone ever dictated your feelings? Was this helpful? What did you do? How did their actions affect the conversation?

8. Can you recall a recent time when someone gave you their undivided attention for a minimum of thirty minutes? How did you feel about that person? Did being heard help you? How?

9. Is there someone in your life who avoids listening to you? How do you feel when you are ignored?

10. Optional Exercise: With a partner, take turns be-

ing the counselor and the friend. Practice the "Do's" of listening; then switch and practice on the "Don'ts." Share your impressions with each other of both situations.

_____ *3*

WHAT IF THEY
WON'T CHANGE?

Behold, I am doing a new thing!
Now it springs forth; do you not perceive
and know it and will you not give heed to it?
ISAIAH 43:19

*I*can't listen to Barbara one more time!" a friend cried in
desperation. "Every time we talk it's the same old
thing—how her husband mistreated her, how her friends
have left her, how miserable she is! I have made suggestion
after suggestion, but it's as if she doesn't even hear me. All
she wants to do is tell me how awful her life is. I don't think
she really wants help!"

Another man shared, "I've been working with Tony for
quite a while now, but I'm beginning to think it's useless.
At first I didn't mind the demands he made on my time,
because I realized that he had a lot of needs. But it's been
six months and I'm still the only Christian he will talk with.
What have I gotten myself into?"

All of us have had experiences with Barbaras and Tonys.

We make ourselves available to listen, encourage, support, and counsel. But the person doesn't change, and we begin to feel used up and frustrated.

How to Assess a Desire for Change

How can you tell if your friend is sincere about changing? What are the steps of change? How can you encourage your friend to make changes? How can you be honest without being offensive?

A Willingness to Do Whatever Is Necessary

Some who ask for help don't want to change; they merely want to get out of pain, or they want someone *else* to change.

Bill was a powerful, masculine, dominant person who came to the office dejected, tearful, and beaten down. He confessed he hadn't been able to sleep or eat since his wife of thirty years had learned of an affair he was having with a woman in his office and had threatened to leave him.

"I'll do anything to get her back!" he sobbed. "I just can't live without her. I'll do whatever she wants, if only she'll give me one more chance!"

He presented the picture of a man who was broken, repentant, and willing to face the problems in his marriage. Six months later, however, he was back in the office again, with the same problem. This time his wife had refused to give him another chance because after she had consented to his moving back into the house, he had resumed the affair with his coworker. He had only wanted to change to the extent that he could have his way. He hadn't really wanted to be changed.

You can gain a sense of your friend's desire to change if

she/he is willing to do whatever it will take to resolve the problem, and if you see specific steps of change that endure over time.

Prayerful and Thoughtful Consideration of Suggestions

Some people only want an audience for their own misery and self-pity. These are the Barbaras you will encounter. Take notice if your friend counters your suggestions with an inordinate number of "Yes, but" excuses, if she always has good reasons why she can't do a particular action you suggest, or if she always gives you reasons why it won't work.

Sometimes these people will go from one friend to another, leaving each burned out and frustrated, often accusing the previous friend of "not understanding." If, however, your friend prayerfully and thoughtfully considers your suggestions, and if she takes even small steps to make changes, you may conclude that her desire to change is strong.

A Focus on the Solution, Not the Problem

People who don't want to change will tend to focus their conversations and energy on the problem and how badly they have been treated, rather than on creative solutions to the problem. While everyone needs some time to work through her feelings about her particular situation, a continual repetition of hurt feelings may indicate that your friend's desire for healing and change is very weak.

What If You See No Change?

What happens if after some time you see no evidence of improvement? What if she seems willing to change but her life shows no evidence of that?

Unclear or Unrealistic Expectations

Before you conclude that your friend doesn't want to change, examine your own expectations. Of course, you will have certain hopes for her; however, your hopes can readily change into unclear or unrealistic expectations of her if she doesn't seem to change quickly or in the manner you would wish. Unrealistic expectations begin when you want a person to progress according to *your own need for results*. You may become tempted to blame her for not progressing more quickly or to doubt her sincerity.

If your friend does not progress according to your need, it will be easy for you to show your disappointment, thus causing her to feel unfair pressure.

One Sunday school teacher confided, "I had such high hopes for Linda. She had always shown such strong leadership skills and an extraordinary knowledge of the Bible. But since her husband has left, she's gotten so involved in other activities that she doesn't even seem interested in God! She's joined an athletic club, a bridge club, and a ballroom dance group. Her finances are getting more and more out of control. I never dreamed she would be like this. I thought, with my help, she would be a great witness of God's strength during crisis. I've tried and tried to point this out to her, but she's just not interested. I'm so disappointed! Now she's even begun to cancel our times together and actually seems to be avoiding me!"

Because this teacher had *expected* her friend to behave in a certain way, she was disappointed and disillusioned when these expectations were not met. Because she did not recognize her *own* needs and expectations, opportunity for ministry was lost.

If you sense that the relationship with your friend is becoming strained, ask God to show you where you may have imposed some of your own needs upon her. If you find that you have done this, ask her forgiveness before you continue counseling, if she is willing to do so.

Just as you may have unrealistic expectations of your friend, you may find that she will develop unrealistic expectations of you. Because of your faith and knowledge, she may expect you to always have answers for her. Because of your resources, she may also expect you to meet more of her needs than you can. She may want you to be "perfect" so that she can place excessive dependence upon you.

One woman told of a problem which she encountered: "I feel a lot of pressure coming toward me from a young woman I am counseling. Although our agreement was to meet once a week, she has begun to ask me to run errands for her and to baby-sit her children. When I don't fulfill her requests, she gets resentful. Lately, I've begun to feel resentful toward her, too. And I feel awful about it!"

If you become aware that your friend is developing unrealistic expectations of you, let her know in a kind manner. You might say, "I believe I need to remind you that the best way I can help you is through counseling, not running errands or babysitting. I know, however, that these are real needs, so could we set a time to pray together and discuss other ways to get those needs met? I believe God will help us."

This will offer a good time for you to talk with her about God as her provider. Share Scripture verses such as Philippians 4:19: "And my God will liberally supply (fill to the full) your every need according to His riches in glory in Christ Jesus." By doing this, you will not be disregarding her needs, nor will you come under the strain of trying to fulfill all of them yourself. You will be helping her to draw close to God, as well as providing her with an avenue for practice in problem solving.

35

Addressing the Problem

If after several months your friend does not appear to solve her problem, and the difficulty is not with unrealistic or unclear expectations, then you may need to gently confront her. You might say, "We've been talking together for a long time. Do you think we've made any progress?" If she is unable to point out ways in which she feels she has progressed, you may want to suggest that you discontinue meeting for awhile. Let her know that you aren't disappointed in her and that each person has her own pace of change. Assure her that you love her and want God's best for her life, and that when her desire is greater, you will be available to meet with her again.

Encourage her to seek God's help in strengthening her desire to change. A good verse to use is Proverbs 16:3, "Roll your works upon the Lord [commit and trust them wholly to Him; He will cause your thoughts to become agreeable to His will, and] so shall your plans be established and succeed." As she begins to give her situation to God, assure her that God is ". . . all the while effectually at work in you [energizing and creating in you the power and desire], both to will and to work for His good pleasure and satisfaction and delight" (Philippians 2:13).

How to Provide a Climate for Change

Sometimes the desire to change is there, but the person just doesn't know how to bring it about in her life. What can you do to help her achieve progress in her situation?

Express Confidence in Her and in God

Point out the strengths you have observed in your friend. Any difficulty she experiences in one aspect of her life does not negate the expertise she may have in others. If she expresses feelings of helplessness, remind her of strengths she may have forgotten. For example, if she is going for a first-time job interview, you might remind her of the organizational skills she has exhibited in her own personal life. If she is fearful, ask her to recall situations in which God eased her mind and made her able to do something that was difficult. Build confidence in her abilities by using your own memory.

These verses will build her up in anxious times:

> I have strength for all things in Christ Who empowers me [I am ready for anything and equal to anything through Him Who infuses inner strength into me; I am self-sufficient in Christ's sufficiency]. (Philippians 4:13)

> Fear not [there is nothing to fear], for I am with you; do not look around you in terror and be dismayed, for I am your God. I will strengthen and harden you to difficulties, yes, I will help you; yes, I will hold you up and retain you with My [victorious] right hand of rightness and justice. (Isaiah 41:10)

Remember Your Friend Has a Right to Her Choices

Remember that your friend has a God-given right to make her own decisions. If you see that your friend is insistent upon making a wrong choice, then let her make her choice, even though the results may be obvious to you.

Although you may attempt to *influence* your friend to do what is right, do not try to coerce her into agreement with you. As Joshua told the Israelites: ". . . choose for yourselves this day whom you will serve . . ." (Joshua 24:15). Give her the same privilege. If you try to insist that she do things your way, you may block a much-needed lesson in her life. Be careful not to take on a God-like position. Many life-changing lessons are only learned through our suffering the consequences of a mistake or sin.

"Your friend may simply need to take time to absorb what she has already experienced and learned. Soaking times are important."

Pray for your friend and be available to listen if she experiences the pain of error. If she is willing, help her define how she went wrong and identify what she has learned. She may want to discuss ways to avoid making the same mistake in the future. No experience is worthless if wisdom is gained from it!

Recognize the Necessity of Plateaus

Carla was distraught. "I don't feel I'm getting anywhere anymore!" she exclaimed. "When I first began counseling, I was changing every day! Lately, I've just seemed stuck! What is wrong?"

As you work with your friend, expect plateaus in her change process. During changes, we tend to progress rapidly for awhile, then to level off for a rest period. Your friend may exert much energy in the initial crisis period, receive some relief, and appear less interested in progressing. She may simply need to take time to absorb what she has already experienced and learned. Soaking times are important. During this time, your primary roles may be to pray and to be available when needed.

Assure her that a time of "soaking" and practice of what she has learned is necessary. Rather than seeing this as backward steps, help her to understand that the change process will be a series of fast growth or change, followed by periods of stabilization.

A plateau period may provide an opportunity for you and your friend to enjoy recreation together. If you continue to maintain contact, even when the need for help may not be as intense, your friend will be less likely to think she had only been a "project" to you, and she will know that you enjoy her as a person.

Be Careful Not to Judge

When we judge someone, we reject, or pass sentence on them. Sometimes we do this without even realizing it. How? Judgments are filled with blame and condemnation. For example, you may find yourself saying, "Well, you asked for it!" or "I think you really brought this on yourself!" Worst of all is, "I tried to warn you, but you didn't listen!"

When your friend repeats the same sin or mistake, it will be difficult not to remind her that you "told her so." Judging, however, separates people from each other. There is sometimes a fine line between judging a person and judging a behavior.

One man said, "I couldn't believe Jim told such a lie! He should never be trusted again!" By that statement, Jim as a person, rather than the specific behavior, was condemned in the eyes of his friend.

You can express sorrow or regret for your friend's action without judging. For example, you might say, "I'm really sorry this has happened," or "I'm sorry you are hurting so badly. How can I help now?" One of the most helpful responses is, "No matter what you have done, God loves you and so do I."

"There is no guarantee that you can tell the truth without offending, but prefacing your statements may soften your words."

If you express concern without judging, your friend will not have to withdraw from you in shame. Then you will have an opening to talk about repentance and restitution (see chapters 9: "Betrayal," and 12: "Guilt").

Remember, Jesus specifically tells us not to judge one another (Matthew 7:1). Such an all-encompassing action is reserved only for God.

How Can I Be Honest with My Friend Without Offending Her?

When you are attempting to maintain a good rapport with your friend, you will naturally want her to like you. Therefore, it is often tempting to try to please her at the expense of helping.

Sandra told me, "My friend asked if I thought she had done the right thing when she emptied her savings account for a new wardrobe. She said that it made her feel so much better to have new clothes, but I knew that overspending was one of her major problems. I realized I made a mistake when I simply told her how good she looked, even adding that I was just glad that she was happy!"

There is no guarantee that you can tell the truth without offending, but prefacing your statements may soften your words. For example, you might say, "I can understand why you did that, and I might have done the same thing, but have you thought about . . . ?" or "It's hard for me to say this, because I know you may be disappointed, but . . ." or "You usually make such good judgments. How did you come to your decision?" Comments such as these may lead your friend to reexamine her decisions or actions, relieving the need for further comment on your part.

It is important to lovingly express the truth. Truth that is not clothed in love may simply create another wound within your friend. Love will cloak the truth in gentleness, and love will empower the truth to make a needed change.

Ask God to show you how to be honest with your friend in a kind and gentle manner. Pray that your words will come at a time in which she can receive them. When your words are given in love, your attitude will cover any mistakes you may make in the telling (Proverbs 10:12).

How Do I Leave the Ultimate Responsibility to God?

Remember that your role is to be a helping friend—not to make your friend change. The responsibility for change rests solely with your friend and upon God. You will be very tempted to take on the responsibility for her change. Therefore, it is important to remember certain facts.

Point Her to Jesus

Keep in mind that your first priority is to point your friend to Jesus. Although she may resist your efforts, preferring to simply have your attention rather than taking the time to seek God, she must learn to get her deepest needs met from Jesus directly, rather than always through you. In this way, she will develop a relationship that will sustain her in situations all of her life.

"Keep in mind that your first priority is to point your friend to Jesus."

Talk with her about the Holy Spirit. Study John 14 and 15 together, explaining how the Holy Spirit is God within her, always with her—her Comforter, Teacher, and Standby. As she comes to realize that the Holy Spirit is the One who took Jesus' place on the earth, and that He is within her, she will be able to look to Him.

Don't Take Responsibility for What She Should Do

You may need to give advice or suggestions, but you should never put yourself in the position of telling your friend what to do. Remind yourself often that she must make her own choices. If you tell her what to do, it will be easy for her to blame you if your solution doesn't work.

Commit Your Friend to the Father

Commit your friend to the Father daily. Remember that He cares for your friend even more than you do (1 Peter 5:7). Say aloud these words from Acts 20:32 for your friend, inserting her name in the passage as follows:

I commit [her name] to God [I deposit her in His charge, entrusting her to His protection and care]. And I commend [her name] to the Word of His grace [to the commands and counsels and promises of His unmerited favor]. It is able to build [her name] up and to give [her rightful] inheritance among all God's set-apart ones (those consecrated, purified, and transformed of soul).

Your role is to offer your friend the Father's love, not to change her. God's role is to work in your friend to save, change, deliver, and heal.

You may never know what effects your friendship will have on your friend. You may never see the full results of the seeds of time, love, and care you planted. But be assured that He who began the good work, of which you were a part, will continue that work in your friend, perfecting it and completing it (Philippians 1:6)!

LIFE APPLICATIONS

1. Have you ever become involved with someone and ended up feeling used? Give an example.

2. Have you ever found yourself becoming angry with someone for continually refusing your suggestions? Why?

3. How do you respond when someone makes unrealistic demands on you?

4. Can you recall a time when someone specifically pointed out your strengths? What was one of them? What effect did this have on you?

5. Is it difficult for you to watch a person make a bad choice? How do you feel? What do you do?

6. Has anyone ever condemned you with their words? What was the result? Did your behavior change? Why or why not?

7. When was someone tactfully honest with you? What did they say or do? Was it helpful?

8. Have you ever told someone what to do and then been blamed for the results? Give an example. How could you have avoided that?

9. Is it easy for you to commit your friend to God, or do you feel like you must change her?

4

MORE WHAT IF'S . . .

When you walk, your steps shall not be hampered [your path will be clear and open]; and when you run, you shall not stumble. Take firm hold of instruction, do not let go; guard her, for she is your life.

PROVERBS 4:12–13

I think I'm ready to begin counseling a friend," the serious, handsome young man said. "I don't feel I have to make my friend change, and I know that God will show me what to do and what to say. But what if . . . ?"

There are always more "what-if" questions when a person begins a new and somewhat frightening relationship or task. The verses quoted above from Proverbs 4:12–13 tell us that instruction causes us to have a clear path so that our steps aren't hampered, and we don't fall into hidden snares. This chapter addresses some questions I have found to arise in friendship-counseling relationships. By considering these issues before you begin to work with your friend, you will be able to avoid many difficulties. With this information, and the guidance of the Holy Spirit, your counseling relationships will be more relaxed and fruitful.

How Can I Keep from Giving Too Much?

When you begin in a counseling relationship, ask God to show you, step by step, just what He is asking you to do. Sometimes, your friend may be asking you for more than what God wants you to do. Go slowly and give yourself time to hear God's instructions. If you feel hesitant about taking the next step, *wait*. The Holy Spirit may be checking your progress in performing this service.

Not everything "good" that you may be asked to do by your friend or others will be your assignment from God. When Paul and Silas planned a trip to preach in Asia, they were "forbidden by the Holy Spirit" (Acts 16:6). The preaching trip was not a wrong thing to do—the people there needed to hear the gospel as much as others did. But God didn't want them going there *at that time*. Be sensitive to the Spirit, as well as to your heart.

When the needs of your friend are great, it is tempting to want to do more than enough. God may ask you to contribute what may seem very little, but do not try to judge its effects. Sometimes, doing less will accomplish more good for your friend in the long run.

Judy was counseling Susan, a young college senior. As the time for exams approached, Susan's fiancé broke their engagement. Since her friend was so distraught, Judy offered to do the research for Susan's term paper. Because she did this, Susan lost the benefit of the experience and knowledge gained from completing her own assignments even under the stress.

When you do more than God instructs you to do, remember that you are being disobedient and that you are actually sinning. Remember that *God* is your friend's strength and that you are only a contributor to her well-being.

How Do I Keep My Friend from Becoming Too Dependent?

One who has been hurt has a great need for love, comfort, and encouragement. Because she has been hurt or experienced loss, your friend may not be willing to trust many people initially. Her emotional needs, combined with your availability and compassion, will make it seem natural for her to rely heavily on you instead of on God or others. This may particularly be true if you are someone who often does too much for others.

Although allowing your friend to depend emotionally upon you for too much support may *appear* to be a kindness because of the initial relief it will provide for her, in the long run it will prove to be a disservice to her. As a human being, you will not be able to meet her deepest needs, nor will you always be available or willing to try. If you let yourself become the only person upon whom she depends, she will become deeply disillusioned at some point.

Janice said, "I really do care about Sandy, but when she gets depressed, I can't do enough for her. She's like a bucket without a bottom! She wants more and more of my time. When I don't give it to her, she manufactures a crisis, or she gets even more depressed. Once she accused me of not even caring, so, of course, I went right over! I don't want to hurt her, but she seems too dependent on me now. What can I do?"

Keep in mind that your first priority is to point your

friend to Jesus. Although she may resist your efforts, prefer-ring to beg for your attention rather than taking the time to seek God, she will grow only if you hold your ground.

You not only need to realize that she may become too dependent on you, but also that you may be tempted to get too dependent or involved with her, thus reinforcing the de-pendency cycle. All of us have dependency needs. God cre-ated us to be dependent, and to live interdependently, rather than in isolation. However, He intended for us to be primarily dependent on Him.

In a counseling relationship, you may find that your own needs of self-worth and adequacy are met as you help your friend. When you begin to define your value as a worthwhile person by helping your friend, you will then be in danger of fostering an unhealthy dependency.

"When you become a 'helper,' you may find yourself experiencing a new sense of power."

Ask the Holy Spirit to guide you as you grow in your relationship with your friend. Have several relationships and encourage your friend to do the same. Don't rely only on one another for counsel, conversation, stimulation, or ministry. Suggest involvement with others, such as a sup-port group. Support groups offer almost immediate rap-port, due to the bond of the Holy Spirit, as well as the commonality of problems and needs. Stay close to God, and value other relationships in your life.

If you begin to feel there is a potential problem with

overdependency, be honest with her about your feelings or concerns. Addressing the issue before it becomes a problem may be initially uncomfortable, but it will prevent future hurt, resentment, and even loss of the friendship later.

What If My Friend Puts Me on a Pedestal?

We all want to be needed, to feel that we can make a valuable contribution to the life of a friend. In fact, this is what ministry is all about. However, when you become a "helper," you may find yourself experiencing a new sense of power. As you give, the lessons you have learned and the knowledge you have will become obvious to you. Your friend may become tempted to see you as more powerful than she and to put you on some kind of pedestal, because of her position of need. If this happens, remind yourself and your friend that each of you is more informed and experienced in certain areas than the other. Consider your friend's sphere of expertise and ask her advice in those areas.

Joe commented, "You know, Jake's marriage is in a terrible mess, but he sure is a good golfer! We've played together a few times, and he's given me a lot of pointers that have helped my game. I think it's important to remind him that he knows more than I do about a lot of things. Just because his marriage is in trouble, he tends to forget about everything else."

Find time to discuss subjects that may be more familiar to your friend than they are to you. Compliment her on any accomplishments she has made. Let her know that you see more in her life than her current problems. Be yourself. Be human. Those who provide counseling often feel that they must appear to "have it all together" in their own lives. By sharing a problem of your own or by admitting to times of confusion, difficulty, or fatigue, you remind yourself, as well as your friend, that you also have needs.

Some counselors become too concerned when they realize how much satisfaction they experience when helping another person. That feeling of gratification is God's way of rewarding you for ministry. The Lord Himself said, "Give and [gifts] will be given to you; good measure, pressed down, shaken together, and running over, will they pour . . ." (Luke 6:38). Joy comes to us when we help another person. So embrace the feeling of joy! It will give you the strength to continue during difficult times.

What If I Overidentify with Certain Problems?

If you are helping a friend with a problem similar to one you have previously experienced, you may find yourself overidentifying with her at times. You may then begin to overinvest emotionally in the outcome and feel anxious yourself. It is also very possible to identify with her so much that *you* become emotionally fatigued. You may become tempted to overcomfort, in order to relieve your own feelings, as well as hers.

Be careful not to interfere with God's work in your friend. Pain is a very effective teacher, and at some point it may be necessary for change to occur.

When you find yourself overidentifying, remember *who* has the problem. Pray for guidance and distance yourself, if necessary, until you regain a balanced perspective. Let your friend know that you have become overconcerned and that you need time to be refreshed. When you do this, you will be providing more opportunity for your friend to find the peace of God. Jesus' words will comfort you both: "Peace I leave with you; My [own] peace I now give and bequeath to you. Not as the world gives do I give to you. Do not let your hearts be troubled, neither let them be afraid. [Stop allowing yourselves to be agitated and disturbed; and do not permit yourselves to be fearful and intimidated and cowardly and unsettled]" (John 14:27).

You may also not be ready to counsel in some areas. For example, if you have recently been through a period of depression or if you have recently lost a family member, then you may not be sufficiently recovered to begin a sustaining relationship with a person experiencing the same situation or problem. Seek counsel from someone else who knows you well before you make a commitment in a situation like that.

How Can I Protect My Time?

Because it is important that you guard your own time, begin setting limits early. Many who are in a crisis are so wrapped up in their own situation that they are not aware of others' needs. You will need to safeguard your time.

For example, if it is inconvenient for you to talk on the telephone after school hours or at work, tell your friend. If there are certain hours when you can be easily available, give her those times. If she calls at a time when you are busy, let her know at the beginning of the conversation that your time is limited, so that you will not have to cut her off. You might say, "I only have a few minutes and cannot really give you my full attention now." Offer to return her call later. If you can, give her a specific time when she can expect to hear from you. Then be sure to call her at the time you promised.

If you thoughtfully define what you are able to give and what you cannot and establish those limits from the beginning, then your counseling relationship will avoid many misunderstandings and snags. Pray for wisdom and direction. Remember that God may not ask you to do as much for your friend as you are able, and He will never ask you to do more than you are able to do!

What About Promises?

Because your friend will probably be experiencing anxiety, it will be tempting to make rash promises, thinking that these will help reduce her anxiety level. Joan told me of finding herself uncomfortably bound by a promise she had made: "I felt so sorry for Cindy! She was absolutely overwhelmed by what had happened. I found myself promising to visit with her twice a week, knowing all the time that I probably couldn't do it. Now I have to go back on my word. I shouldn't have made that promise. I was just trying to help, and I got carried away."

When you begin counseling, it is important to be reasonably certain that you can deliver what you offer. It is always better to offer less than more. As Jesus said, "For which of you, wishing to build a farm building, does not first sit down and calculate the cost [to see] whether he has sufficient means to finish it? Otherwise, when he has laid the foundation and is unable to complete [the building], all who see it will begin to mock and jeer at him" (Luke 14:28–29).

When you make rash promises and cannot keep them, resentment is bound to occur. Pray carefully about your commitments.

How Do I Accept Gratitude?

We all like to be appreciated, but when we take the gratitude of a friend too seriously, we can also become tempted to take credit for their progress. Always remember that your friend's progress is due to the help of the Holy Spirit working in and through you.

Rachel exclaimed, "I feel so awkward when Paula thanks me over and over for my help. I don't know how to respond. How can I receive her appreciation in a gracious manner that does not distract from the Holy Spirit?"

You may offer these responses: "I'm so glad that I could be of help to you," or "It's nice of you to tell me," or "I thank God for the time we've had together. I've also learned a lot! It's meant a lot to me, too."

What About Lending Money and Giving Gifts?

Lending money can cause confusion in your counseling relationship. If you have the financial resources and feel led by God to fill a need, it is best to *give* money rather than lend it. If your friend finds herself unable to return the money to you, she will feel guilty and awkward. You may also begin to question her integrity, and distrust can result.

One man said, "I loaned my friend some money when he promised he could repay it at the end of the week. That day came, and he never mentioned it. I didn't mention it, either, because I really didn't need it then. The next week, he offered an excuse and promised to pay me in two weeks. I assured him that it would be all right, but he didn't pay me then either. Each time we meet now, the first thing he does is apologize for not paying me the money he owes! It has become very awkward. I've even told him to just forget about the money, but he keeps assuring me that he wants to pay me back. This issue has put a strain on our relationship."

Gifts of money or other articles are best kept to a minimum. Large amounts or unusual gifts can create a sense of obligation for your friend and become more of a burden than a relief.

If there is a true financial need, and you feel led to help, you might want to consider benevolence funds in your church or community, and suggest that your friend contact those sources.

How Will I Know If My Friend Needs Professional Help?

If your friend does not appear to be improving, even though she is working cooperatively with you, suggest that she consider professional help. In some cases, prolonged depression or anxiety can be due to a physiological problem. Prolonged stress can cause many types of physical problems to occur which may affect her emotional system. There may be emotional problems due to deep-seated hurts from the past which you and she have not been able to discuss.

If your friend seems to become despondent or talks about suicide, it is important that you take her seriously. Tell her directly that you are very concerned. Assure her of your faithfulness to her, and emphasize the importance of her life to God, as well as to you (see chapter 5: "Depression," for more information about suicide prevention).

It may comfort your friend if you offer to go with her to a doctor or a counselor. Let her know that you are not abandoning her but that you will still remain available to serve as a support.

Other Considerations

You will need to consider several factors both before you decide to counsel a friend and while you are in a counseling relationship.

Have Others Pray for You

Being careful to guard confidentiality, ask someone to pray for you as you work with your friend. Every worker gets tired during a crisis.

The book of Exodus tells of a battle between Israel and Amalek. When Moses held up his hand, holding the rod of God, Israel prevailed; but when he lowered his hand, Amalek had the advantage (Exodus 17:8–13). As the day progressed, Moses became tired and weak, and Aaron and Hur held up his arms "so his hands were steady until the going down of the sun" (Exodus 17:12).

Let others pray for you. This will benefit not only you and your friend, but the people who are praying!

Stay Rested

At times Jesus needed to be away from people and to isolate Himself with His Father. If Jesus needed a time of refreshing, so do we. When you begin to feel drained, give yourself a break. If you allow yourself to become exhausted, you may find that you will fail your friend at the most crucial time.

Both mental and physical rest are important. Paul warned us to "be constantly renewed in the spirit of your mind [having a fresh mental and spiritual attitude]" (Ephesians 4:23).

Unless you take time for rest as you work with your friend, your mind can become so overstimulated that you will not be able to maintain a clear, calm state of being.

Maintain Good Health Habits

Your body will often warn you when you are mentally and emotionally overloaded. Healthy eating habits, regular exercise, and rest will ensure that you will have the mental and physical strength and stamina necessary for giving to others.

You must also learn to pace yourself. Human zeal can often conflict with the pace of the Holy Spirit. Just as runners must pace themselves for the endurance race, we must discipline our natural minds with openness to the move of God's Spirit. It can be difficult to get into stride with His pace, but through prayer and surrender, it can be done.

Throw Off Weights

If you are going to complete a difficult course with your friend, you must make sure that you do not carry extra weight.

Regrets. Regrets can hinder your relationship with your friend. Accept the fact that you will make some mistakes as you counsel your friend. You may say the wrong thing at the wrong time, or you may offend her. You may find that some of your suggestions are not helpful. When this happens, simply admit your mistake, apologize, and work with your friend on another alternative.

Paul understood this, saying his answer was by "forgetting what lies behind and straining forward to what lies ahead, I press on toward the goal to win the [supreme and heavenly] prize to which God in Christ Jesus is calling us upward" (Philippians 3:13–14).

Regret and sorrow are heavy weights. Deal with them and cast them away from you as quickly as possible.

Sins. Sins are also heavy weights. If you have unconfessed sins in your life, it will be easy to be preoccupied or distracted. Confess your sins daily. Come before God and present yourself as David did when he said, "Wash me thoroughly [and repeatedly] from my iniquity and guilt and

cleanse me and make me wholly pure from my sin! . . .
Create in me a clean heart, O God, and renew a right,
persevering, and steadfast spirit within me" (Psalm 51:2,
10).

Study God's Word for Your Own Life

When you are working with a friend, it is sometimes easy to
let your Bible study begin to revolve around her needs. One
Bible teacher related, "I realized that I have been spending
all of my study time preparing for my classes. I can't remember the last time I just sat down with my Bible and
opened it just for myself! I forgot how much I need strength
from God's Word, too."

Keep your mind girded up with God's Word on an ongoing basis. Fill your mind with His Word during the easier
times so that you will be able to more readily recall it during difficulties. Remember that He knows the future and
will prepare you for difficulties.

Be Aware That Satan Is at Work

The apostle Peter warned: "That enemy of yours, the devil,
roams around like a lion roaring [in fierce hunger], seeking
someone to seize upon and devour" (1 Peter 5:8). Do not
underestimate Satan's desires to destroy your friend and
you. (For further information see chapter 17 on spiritual
warfare.)

If difficulties begin to occur between you and your
friend, look for the source of the problem rather than blaming her. The works of the enemy are listed in Galatians 5.
At times it is more effective not to address an issue with
your friend directly but to attack the problem through
prayer, binding Satan from further interference.

I led a group for women, for a while, with a friend.
Each time we would begin a new group for women, one of

us would get angry at the other for no apparent reason. This would usually occur immediately before the group members were to arrive. This, of course, was not a good time for the group leaders to be irritated with each other!

The first several times this happened, we tried to talk about the "problem" but found that usually we made the situation more intense than it had been originally! Finally, we realized that the "problem" was coming from Satan, attempting to get us upset with each other to prevent us from working effectively in the Spirit with the group.

"Keep your mind girded up with God's Word on an ongoing basis. Fill your mind with His Word during the easier times so that you will be able to more readily recall it during difficulties."

When we began praying against the work of Satan instead of talking to each other about the "problem," the "problem" ceased to exist!

Always Remember That God Has Control

When tragedies occur or difficulties seem to compound and continue endlessly, do not forget that God really does have control.

Pray as David did:

My soul, wait only upon God and silently submit to Him; for my hope and expectation are from Him. He only is my Rock and my Salvation; He is my Defense and my Fortress, I shall not be moved. With God rests my salvation and my glory; He is my Rock of unyielding strength and impenetrable hardness, and my refuge is in God! Trust in, lean on, rely on, and have confidence in Him at all times, you people; pour out your hearts before Him. God is a refuge for us (a fortress and a high tower). (Psalm 62:5–8)

Remember, when things seem out of control, your Father is in control. You can count on Him to rescue and see you through any trouble. As you work with your friend, trust Him to help you both. Pour out your heart to Him. Receive His strength. He knows the future, and He will act on her behalf.

LIFE APPLICATIONS

1. Why would God ask you not to help?

2. Can you recall a time when you ignored God's instructions, became involved, and realized you had made a mistake? What did you do?

3. Almost all of us have allowed someone to become too dependent on us. When did this happen to you? What did you learn?

4. Have you ever become too dependent on someone else? Was this helpful?

5. Have you ever been a member of a support group? How did it help you?

6. Have you ever felt the discomfort of being on a pedestal? What were your two main feelings?

7. What are some areas in which you may not be ready to counsel due to recent experiences of your own?

8. What time of day can you be most available?

9. Has lending money ever been a problem to you? What happened?

10. Are you familiar with professional resources in your area, such as battered women's shelters, financial aid, health support systems, etc.?

11. Can you recall a time when you were exhausted and a crisis occurred? What would have helped you?

12. Has someone who meant well ever given you the wrong advice? Have you forgiven them? Why or why not?

PART TWO

THE
HELPING
HEART

5

DEPRESSION

Hope deferred makes the heart sick . . .
PROVERBS 13:12

I feel so sad and hopeless. I just can't make myself do things anymore. Everything is such an effort. I cry over the least little thing that happens. I can't sleep, and I can't concentrate on anything. I don't know what is wrong. Can you help me?"

This letter from a friend reflects the feelings of the majority of people alive today. Most have either experienced or will experience a mild to severe period of depression during their lives. It has been estimated that more than ten million Americans each year suffer from this condition. None of us is exempt from the circumstances of life that create depression. Depression is more than a passing mood of feeling blue or down. Depression can be debilitating and overwhelming. How can you help a friend who is depressed? What are the different kinds of depression? What are some of the causes? How can you offer your friend hope?

Is Your Friend Depressed?

Depression can wear many faces, but usually a person who is depressed will exhibit a variety of feelings, behaviors, and physical complaints. The following checklist will help you determine if your friend is suffering from depression:

Feelings:

- Feels sad and hopeless
- Is apathetic and bored
- Not interested in normal activities
- Feels guilty
- Feels worthless and inadequate
- Blames self
- Feels no one cares
- Is easily irritated
- Expects the worst
- Feels angry (may or may not express this)

Behaviors:

- Withdraws from others
- May neglect appearance
- Doesn't engage in routine activities
- May stay in bed all day
- Cannot do ordinary work
- Supersensitive to noise

- Makes negative statements ("No one cares about me.")
- May discuss suicide ("I wish I were dead.")
- Cries easily for no apparent reason
- Has many complaints
- Unable to concentrate
- Is indecisive
- Easily distracted

Physical Symptoms:

- Headaches
- Weight loss or gain
- Restlessness and agitation
- Many aches and pains
- Sleep problems
- Stomach problems
- Dizzy spells
- Chest sensations

If your friend has many of these symptoms, she may be suffering from the effects of depression.

Types of Depression

Through some examples, let us examine the various types of depression.

Major Depression

James was a man in his early forties whose wife contacted me for help. A very active, energetic and caring man, James had become withdrawn, angry, and apathetic over the last months. He had begun missing work, had quit going to church, was ignoring the children, and had stopped working out with his friend. Lately he had begun talking about his life insurance policies and making comments such as, "If I weren't here, you would need to. . . ." While his work had been more stressful lately, James didn't seem to be under severe pressure. What was happening to her husband?

James was suffering from major depression, the most severe, as well as one of the most common types, affecting more than five and one half million Americans each year. This type of depression is overwhelming and persistent, frequently lasting at least two weeks but usually longer. Symptoms are intense and are a dramatic change from the person's usual behavior. Thoughts of suicide and death are not uncommon.

Situational Depression

Situational depression may be mild or severe, but it is the result of some event or stress in a person's life.

Sue came to the office weeping and in acute distress. As we talked, she confided that she and her boyfriend of four years had broken up. Although it had been several months, she just couldn't seem to get her life back in order.

"I miss him so much," she cried. "I know it was for the best, but I just can't get used to his absence. I can't sleep; I don't want to eat; I don't enjoy my friends. All I do is think about him and cry. My work is suffering, and I know my friends are worried about me. What can I do to get through this time?"

While situational depression can be as severe as the other types, it lifts when the stressor goes away, or the problem is solved.

Manic-Depressive Illness

Manic-depressive illness, or bipolar depression, is characterized by a series of either highs and lows, or one of the two. A person in a "manic" phase will not seem depressed as we have defined depression, but she will display characteristics such as decreased need for sleep, extreme talkativeness, racing thoughts, distractibility, and extreme activity. Usually, the person has an inflated view of herself, and many times she will show excessive involvement in pleasurable activities which have a high potential for painful consequences, such as unrestrained buying sprees or foolish business investments.

"None of us is exempt from the circumstances of life that create depression."

Larry, a businessman in his early forties, appeared to be the picture of success, energy, and congeniality. He had several business interests, was well-liked in the community, and was always ready for a new challenge. His wife, however, became very concerned about him when he emptied their savings on a risky land venture.

She confided, "He has always been careful about our

retirement money and the children's college funds, but lately, nothing I say to him seems to penetrate. About two months ago, he seemed depressed. Then, all of a sudden, he changed. At first I thought it was another woman. But he's never been unfaithful to me. I'm worried that he's not sleeping, he's not taking care of his usual business, and he just seems driven. What can I do to help him? He doesn't think anything is wrong. He says it's the best he's felt in years! But I just know something is wrong!"

Chronic Depression

Many people suffer from a milder, but chronic form of depression called *dysthymia*. In this type, the person experiences long periods of low mood and depressive symptoms. This depression can last for years and is sometimes experienced as a low-grade depression. Often people with this type of depression may not be aware that something is wrong because they are so accustomed to being down.

Joe came for help because "I just don't feel good. Nothing really is wrong or has happened. I'm just dissatisfied. I feel like my emotions are numb and have been maybe all of my life. There's got to be more to life than this. I want the 'abundant life' Jesus talked about, but I don't know how to experience it. I love God, but something is missing."

As we talked, Joe told a story of childhood abuse. He had learned to numb his feelings in order to cope with the verbal and physical abuse he suffered. He had been depressed as a child, and he was a depressed adult. Never having known what it was like *not* to be depressed, he didn't recognize that what he was experiencing was depression until he began feeling better.

Another type of chronic depression is *cyclothymia*. This

differs from dysthymia in that the person experiences periods of feeling "high" as well as periods of feeling "low." It is similar to the manic-depressive type, but not as severe or extreme, although the extreme mood shifts can be chronic and recurrent.

Cindy was referred for counseling by her physician who was worried about the mood changes he had observed in her over the last few years. Cindy related, "For the past several years, I have thought at times I was going crazy. I go from feeling on top of the world and that I can do anything to feeling like a failure. Nothing seems to happen; my mood just changes. It scares me, because I never know what I can expect of myself. I'm getting ready to start a new job, but I'm worried that I won't be able to function."

Causes of Depression

As you work with others, you will need to help them to identify the underlying causes of the depression. While there will be many things you can have your friend do that will alleviate her symptoms, it is important that the root problem be addressed. As you work with a friend who is depressed, ask God to show you the roots of her depression.

Physical Causes

Some cases of depression are due to physical causes. These can include chemical imbalances, tumors, diseases, as well as effects of medications. Diet, amount of exercise, amount of sleep, and general physical health are all contributors to general mood and a feeling of well-being.

Sherry had many physical problems for which she took a number of medications. About a month after her last surgery, she told her doctor, "I'm feeling better physically, but emotionally I'm just a wreck. I feel so depressed all the time, and I'm so easily irritated by Rick and the children. I don't know what is wrong with me!"

Much to Sherry's surprise, her doctor told her that feeling depressed was a common reaction to the medicines she was taking. Having that knowledge helped both her and her husband to deal with the feelings.

You may want to consider physical causes as the basis of your friend's depression. Has she had a medical check-up recently? Is she taking any medications? Is she in good health? Is she eating a balanced diet? Does she get regular exercise? What physical factors could be influencing the way she is feeling?

Situations and Stressors

Depression can also be caused by a particular, precipitating event or stressor. A loss of any kind (loss of job, divorce, a relationship), a major life change (retirement, children leaving home, a new career), a disappointment, or an unrealized hope can cause a person to feel depressed. Depression caused by situations or stressors usually dissipates when the situation or the stressor is resolved.

Often depression follows a great achievement or victory. After a great effort, we are emotionally vulnerable and physically exhausted. It is easy to become depressed in the aftermath of overcoming an obstacle. God's great prophet Elijah also experienced fatigue, discouragement, fear, and depression after winning a great spiritual victory (1 Kings 18–19).

Ask your friend when she began feeling depressed. Were there any changes in her life just before she began feeling depressed? Any major changes in the past six months? Is there anything she is particularly worried about at the present? Ask her to describe her relationships with others. Does the way she feels now remind her of anything? What was going on at this time last year or two years ago? How is her life different now compared to before the depression began? What positive changes have been in her life? What has happened in her life spiritually? Were there any achievements or victories preceding her depression?

Childhood Hurts

Much chronic depression is the result of events usually associated with childhood hurts. While there are many types of hurts, they most often fall into categories of neglect or abuse.

Neglect. When a child doesn't receive the emotional or physical nurturing she needs from her parents, she may come to believe that she will never receive what she needs. This sense of hopelessness and helplessness sets the stage for chronic, persistent, low-grade depression.

Anne was a single woman in her thirties who came for therapy seeking help with a career change. She was a pleasant young woman, but she always appeared rather sad. When questioned about depression, she claimed she didn't feel depressed, but added, "But of course, I never feel happy either."

Anne had been the oldest of four children. Both of her parents had worked, and much of the care of her brothers and sisters had fallen on her young shoulders.

"I don't ever remember getting hugs from my mother or dad. They were just never there. When Mom was home, she always had so much to do, and she needed me to help her. Sometimes I felt as if I were the mother instead of the child. I began to feel ashamed of needing attention from my parents. My role was to give—not to receive. I think I've always been angry about that, but I didn't know what to do with it. It's hard for me to receive now; I don't trust people very much. I don't expect much either. I don't think I'll ever get what I need. Maybe I *am* depressed," she concluded.

You will want to ask your friend what kind of relationship she had with her mother and father. Were her emotional/physical needs met as a child? What was her role in the family? Does she have difficulty trusting others? What is the biggest need she senses in her life now? What is her relationship with God the Father? Does she believe He will take care of her and supply her needs?

Abuse. Margaret was a woman in her sixties who had been bothered by depression and suicidal feelings throughout her adult life. She had resisted counseling for years, because she was afraid of the anger that might surface if she ever talked about her past.

Sexually molested by an older brother when she was thirteen, she told her mother, who was horrified that Margaret would "make up such an awful thing" about her brother. At that point, Margaret decided she was a bad person and vowed never to tell anyone again. She married to escape an increasingly unbearable home situation, but after her marriage, her husband physically abused her and later subjected her to sexual abuse by other men. This confirmed to her the fact that she was bad. She repressed the anger she felt toward those who had hurt her, turning it inward on herself. She wanted help with her depression, but she was afraid of looking at her past. Finally, after fifty years of desperation, she decided to take action and came for counseling.

When a person has been abused, the anger felt toward the abusers may be directed inward, resulting in depression. The person may also believe she is a bad person who

72

deserved the abuse, is to blame for the abuse, and thus doesn't deserve happiness. All of these are ingredients for chronic depression.

It is important to discuss her relationship with her parents. Is there a history of abuse, including emotional abuse, in the family? Listen carefully as she talks about her family. Many people don't know they were abused. They think all families are like their own. Does she believe she was not good enough? Does she believe the abuse was her fault, that she deserved to be mistreated, that she was a bad child? Does she have a history of self-destructive behaviors? Does she have difficulty trusting others? Does she have a bad temper? (See chapter 10: "Abuse.")

Disobedience and Unconfessed Sin

David observed, "Blessed (happy, fortunate, to be envied) is the man to whom the Lord imputes no iniquity and in whose spirit there is no deceit. When I kept silence [before I confessed], my bones wasted away through my groaning all the day long" (Psalm 32:2–3).

When a person actively disobeys God and allows unconfessed sin in her life, the inevitable result will be agitation and depression. Guilt results from sin; unconfessed sin and an unrepentant heart lead to the depression caused by a guilty conscience.

Although other causes of depression may be apparent in your friend's life, help her to examine her heart for known sin. The best treatment in the world for depression cannot rid her of a guilty conscience. Only God can do that through Jesus.

Offer your friend the hope of forgiveness: "If we [freely] admit that we have sinned and confess our sins, He is faithful and just (true to His own nature and promises) and will forgive our sins [dismiss our lawlessness] and [continuously] cleanse us from all unrighteousness [everything not in conformity to His will in purpose, thought, and action]" (1 John 1:9).

Ask gentle but probing questions to help your friend deal with unconfessed sin. Does she knowingly engage in any sin? Is there any unconfessed sin in her life for which she has not received forgiveness? Does she feel guilty? Is she able to pray? Does she feel close to God? Is there anything for which she feels God will not forgive her? (See chapter 12: "Guilt.")

An Ungrateful Attitude

"A happy heart is good medicine and a cheerful mind works healing, but a broken spirit dries up the bones" (Proverbs 17:22). Have you ever noticed that certain people leave you feeling drained and weary, while you feel joyful and full around others? People with negative, ungrateful attitudes rob us and themselves of the joy and wonder of God's provision.

Does your friend have an ungrateful heart? Does she complain frequently? Is she happy for the blessings of others, or do they make her envious or angry?

A Spirit of Depression

Sometimes Satan sends an assignment of depression against a person to hinder or distract her. A spirit of depression will prevent your friend from experiencing the power, love, joy, and peace that God gives to all His children. As you counsel, be aware that the battle is not only in the mind, but also in the spiritual realm.

If a person is depressed for no apparent reason, a spirit of depression may be involved. A person under attack by Satan doesn't understand why she feels down, as if she has no control.

If you sense your friend is under the influence of a spirit of depression, ask God for discernment. Talk to a mature Christian or your pastor who is experienced in spiritual warfare. Pray for guidance. If your impression continues to be confirmed, ask your friend if you can pray with her about any spirits of depression that may be present.

Remember that the name of Jesus is the Name above all names and that "in (at) the name of Jesus every knee should (must) bow, in heaven and on earth and under the earth" (Philippians 2:10). When you pray for your friend in the name of Jesus, pray that all spirits not of God will be prevented from harassing her. (For further information on spiritual warfare, see chapter 17.)

What to Do When Someone Is Suicidal

If your friend expresses a wish to die or says things such as, "I can't go on"; "Everyone would be better off without me around"; or "I wish I were dead," take her seriously. It is better to overreact to a suicidal threat than to discount it and underact.

When she talks to you, *don't try to tell her all the advantages of being alive.* Instead, *acknowledge her feelings of hopelessness and despair* in a loving way, by saying, "I know you are hurting," or "I know it seems that way to you now." Try to communicate to her confidence, caring, and hope. Let her know that you are with her, that God loves her, that He will never leave her, and that you care for her and love her.

As you talk with your friend, you will need to *assess the likelihood of her hurting herself* in some way. The following questions can help you determine if your friend is at high risk for a suicide attempt. The more "yes" answers you have, the higher the risk of a suicide gesture.

75

- Does she think suicide is the only way out?

- Does she have a definite, workable suicide plan? Is she vague ("I'm going to drive off the bridge"), or does she have a specific method in mind ("I'm going to take my entire prescription of Valium")?

- Does she have access to the means? For example, if she says she is going to shoot herself, does she have access to a gun?

- Is there a history of drug or alcohol abuse? Is she currently using substances?

- Does she have a history of previous suicidal attempts?

- Has she had a significant life-disturbing event in the last six months?

- Has she experienced a significant loss within the last two years?

- Is she experiencing severe health problems?

- Does she have an intense need to achieve?

- Has she begun "putting her affairs in order"?

- Has her mood improved drastically, as if she feels relieved?

If there are high-risk factors present, you will need to *take steps to protect your friend*. Talk to her husband, parents, roommate, a neighbor. Make sure she has access to nothing with which to hurt herself. Have someone with her at all times until the crisis is past.

Get her to talk to a professional as soon as possible. Don't try to handle this by yourself. Get all the help that is available. Talk with your friend about her possible need for short-term hospitalization. She may be opposed to this, but if you feel the risk is significant, you may have to insist. A trained mental health professional can be of great assistance in this matter.

Don't try to reason with your friend at this point. Take steps to protect her.

Ways to Help

If your friend is not suicidal, you can take certain steps to help her with the problem of depression.

Assure Her That Depression Is Common

David wrote the following during a time of depression in his life:

> I am restless and distraught in my complaint and must moan. . . . My heart is grievously pained within me, and the terrors of death have fallen upon me. Fear and trembling have come upon me; horror and fright have overwhelmed me. And I say, Oh, that I had wings like a dove! I would fly away and be at rest. (Psalm 55:2, 4–6)

It is normal during a period of great distress to be upset and want to "fly away and be at rest!"

One woman with whom I counseled confided, "I was so afraid to come to counseling. I just knew you would think I was a hopeless case—or even worse, that I had no reason to feel like I felt! When you told me that anyone in my situation would feel depressed, I was so relieved! I felt that at last someone understood, that I wasn't so weird after all!"

Let your friend know that you understand that her feelings are natural. Be careful not to say, "You shouldn't feel that way." Whatever a person feels is what she is feeling and nothing more. As you accept her feelings, she will also be able to accept them and to deal with them.

Let Her Know It Is Not a Sin to Be Depressed

Some people have the mistaken idea that it is a sin to be depressed. If your friend believes this, she will try to deny her feelings and thus cut herself off from any kind of help from God.

Let her know that you are not disappointed in her for feeling depressed. It might be helpful to remind her that Jesus experienced similar distress before He was crucified. Matthew records the incident:

> Then Jesus went with them to a place called Gethsemane, and He told His disciples, Sit down here while I go over yonder and pray. And taking with Him Peter and the two sons of Zebedee, *He began to show grief and distress of mind and was deeply depressed.* Then He said to them, *My soul is very sad and deeply grieved, so that I am almost dying of sorrow.* Stay here and keep awake and keep watch with Me. (Matthew 26:36–38, emphasis added)

Jesus expressed His feelings of grief, sorrow, distress, and depression. He knows how your friend feels (Hebrews 2:17–18; 4:15–16).

Help Her to Identify the Root Problem

Get information about her physical condition. Make sure that she is physically well and that the cause of her depression is not physiological. Encourage her to talk with her physician about the value of short-term medication to help her with her depression. This can effectively help a person feel well enough to begin working on her problem.

If the problem seems to be situational in nature, help her problem solve. Help her to form a plan. What can she do? What has she already done? What are some small steps she can take immediately? Set small, easily achievable goals, and encourage her at each step she takes.

Identify the areas in which she has no control. Help her to release those areas to God and to entrust Him with that aspect of the problem. (See the "How to Cast a Care" section in chapter 7: "Fear and Worry.")

"Some people have the mistaken idea that it is a sin to be depressed."

If the depression is stemming from hurts from the past, help her to do what she can to receive emotional healing. If she has been abused or neglected, she will need time to begin her healing process. Pray for wisdom and direction. At this point, you may want to refer her to a professional counselor. You may also wish to work with her through books available on the subject. I recommend my book, *My Father's Child: Help and Healing for the Victims of Emotional, Sexual, and Physical Abuse* (Brentwood, TN: Wolgemuth and Hyatt, 1988). Above all, let her know that help is available and that you will stand by her as she works through the issues of the past. (See chapter 10: "Abuse.")

If the depression is due to disobedience and unconfessed sin, lead her in a prayer of confession and help her see what changes she needs to make. Help her identify what led her into the sin and ways she can avoid the same pitfalls in the future. Encourage her to make changes in her life, with the help of God. Hold her accountable to her decision in a loving, supportive way.

If the depression is rooted in an ungrateful attitude, help her to practice having a grateful heart. Encourage her to confess her ingratitude as a sin and to ask God to give her a grateful heart. Have her begin keeping a daily list of things for which she is thankful. Have her begin sharing these things with others.

If the depression stems from a satanic spirit of depression, pray with your friend for deliverance. Learn all that you can about spiritual warfare and how to stay alert. Help her to identify her areas of vulnerability and teach her about the armor of a Christian and the weapons available to combat the forces of Satan. (See chapter 17 on spiritual warfare.)

Get Your Friend Moving

When a person is depressed, the last thing she wants to do is to get moving, yet this is one of the best actions she can take for herself. Many studies have shown that physical activity stimulates chemicals in the brain that are antagonistic to depression.

Encourage your friend to begin an exercise program. If that seems too monumental, start with suggesting that she do just one thing differently to get out of her rut. This can be something as small as eating in a different place than usual.

Try to get your friend to add one enjoyable activity to her day. Suggest that she include at least one activity with another person, with the goal of increasing her contact with others.

Encourage her to do something for someone else. This can be anything from sending a note to a friend to baking a cake. Becoming involved with others and their needs will help her expand her vision and get a better perspective on her own problems.

Encourage her to join a group of some sort. Invite her to your church or women's group. Join an aerobics class with her. Get her involved with others.

The Miracle of Hope

The greatest gift you can give to a depressed friend is the hope that is found in Jesus. Unless your friend has a relationship with Him, no amount of activity, medicine, encouragement, or friendship will fill the vacuum in her life. Wise King Solomon noted that God "has planted eternity in men's hearts and minds [a divinely implanted sense of a purpose working through the ages which nothing under the sun but God alone can satisfy]" (Ecclesiastes 3:11). Jesus is the Hope that satisfies the longing soul. Without that hope, the heart is sick (Proverbs 13:12). Does your friend know Jesus as her Savior and Friend? Has she committed her life to Him? Does she have a relationship with Him?

Striving to help yourself or another person without the help of God is futile. God alone can do for us what we can never do for ourselves. He alone can change our hearts and our attitudes and bring healing into the deepest parts of our minds, spirits, and bodies.

With God, all things are possible. Healing is available. Jesus came to "bind up and heal the brokenhearted, to proclaim liberty to the [physical and spiritual] captives and the opening of the prison and of the eyes to those who are bound . . . to give them an ornament . . . of beauty instead of ashes, the oil of joy instead of mourning, the garment [expressive] of praise instead of a heavy, burdened, and failing spirit" (Isaiah 61:1, 3).

The miracle of hope—the ultimate cure for depression—is found in a close relationship with Jesus. As you work together, offer your friend this gift of hope.

LIFE APPLICATION _____

1. Have you ever experienced any of the symptoms of depression? What were they? Did you realize you were depressed? Do you know why you were depressed?

2. With which of the types of depression are you the most familiar?

3. Have you ever felt ashamed for being depressed? Is your attitude toward those who are depressed one of compassion or condemnation?

4. Discuss with the group the various causes of depression. With which can you relate? Are there any causes of depression that you think you would have trouble dealing with?

5. Have you ever known anyone who tried to kill herself? Have you ever felt like "ending it all"? What do you believe about suicide?

6. What would you do if your friend told you she had decided everyone would be "better off without me"?

7. What are some things you can do when you are counseling with a friend who is depressed?

6

ANGER

When angry, do not sin; do not ever let
your wrath (your exasperation, your fury
or indignation) last until the sun goes down.

EPHESIANS 4:26

I don't know what's been wrong with me lately. I'm just so
irritable! I snap at everyone around me!"

"I feel like I'm about to explode inside. This pressure
just keeps building! I'm afraid I'm going to hurt one of my
kids if I don't do something about this!"

"I'm so ashamed! I feel so angry and I know that's
wrong. I feel like a failure as a Christian."

Anger mystifies many of us. Often we find ourselves upset for no apparent reason, or overreacting to seemingly
trivial incidents. We "act out" our anger in many ways.
Some of us become depressed, turning the anger toward
ourselves. Some become verbally or physically abusive,
turning the anger toward others. Some deny feelings and
bottle them up, becoming walking time-bombs.

A person who is angry can appear depressed, tired, agitated, irritable, critical, aggressive, or even lethargic. But

what is anger? What are its causes? How can you help others with their anger?

What Is Anger?

Many fear anger, because anger is usually an intense feeling characterized by tremendous energy. Have you ever seen anyone who was so angry she was shaking, red in the face, or clenching her fists?

Anger rarely remains a passive, inactive feeling. On the contrary, anger is a reservoir of energy. The Bible describes anger as "an overwhelming flood" (Proverbs 27:4). The energy of anger may be evident, or it may be repressed. Anger that remains underground is as powerful as that which can be seen. And anger takes a lot of energy to maintain!

Why do we get angry? One of the reasons anger consumes so much energy is because anger is a cover-up for other emotions! Anger is always a *secondary* emotion. *Anger is the person's response to a different feeling.* Sometimes the person is unaware of the feeling fueling her anger. Identifying and understanding feelings that are the hidden activators of anger will help you provide your friend with tools for dealing with her anger.

Anger results from *hurt, fear, or frustration*. Can you recall a time when someone hurt your feelings? Was your first response to work out the hurt, or was it anger? All of us have had the experience of being worried—a lost child, a friend or spouse who is late—and expressing that fear as anger as soon as the wayward person appeared! And how do many of us react when we run out of gas or have a flat tire? Don't most of us, when frustrated and helpless, express irritation and anger? Although these varied feelings may all be expressed as anger, you must help the person deal with the causes.

But I Don't Know Why I'm Angry—I Just Am!

The first step in helping a person to deal with her anger must be identifying the primary emotion and problem. Many of us are unable to identify or describe what *feeling* lies behind our anger, because often we are unaware of our emotions. You will need to think of yourself as a detective, sorting through the various clues the person presents in search of the culprit emotion.

> **"Anger is always a secondary emotion. Anger is the person's response to a different feeling."**

I had been seeing Julie for several months. She had come from a very rigid, unexpressive, "proper" family where children were "to be seen and not heard." She had learned at an early age to keep her feelings to herself. Not only had she been trained not to verbalize negative feelings such as hurt or disappointment, she had also been punished for the expression of positive feelings. She recounted an incident in which she had been chosen by her teacher to represent her school at a local writers' contest. Knowing how her parents valued education, she knew they would be thrilled and excited for her. She ran into the house after school, dancing about, exclaiming proudly, "Mother!

Mother! Where are you? I have the most wonderful news! My story was chosen for the contest!" Distancing herself from Julie, her mother sternly corrected her, "It is not seemly for a young lady to raise her voice or to brag on herself." Ten-year-old Julie was crushed.

You will encounter a lot of Julies—men and women who have been taught to keep their emotions under tight control—who have learned to conceal their emotions even from themselves. Be patient as you help them identify the painful feelings behind their anger.

Getting to the Root

Begin by asking your friend to recall when she first began to feel angry. If she can't pinpoint a specific incident, ask her to describe what has been happening in her life recently. Listen for tension in her voice. Watch for expression of stress in her body language as she talks.

Patricia, a young woman in her twenties whom I had counseled for several months, remarked in one of her early sessions, "I'm angry all the time. I don't know why. My friends say I'm irritable and don't smile much. I know I get really mad about little things that don't matter a lot, especially at work. Can you help me with my anger?"

As she shared her background, she spoke of her stepfather, a domineering, critical, intimidating man who had sexually and verbally abused her during her teenage years. As she began to face her buried feelings, her present anger began to diminish. Her overreactions to stress were less frequent. The change was noticeable even to her friends.

One morning, however, she arrived for her appointment very distressed, complaining of irritability, moodiness, and anger. We talked about what had been going on in her life that week. She recounted a confrontation with her boss. As she spoke, she realized that she had been angry since that meeting.

"What about that meeting upset you?" I asked.

"I realized that no matter what I did, it wasn't going to be good enough for him. He was determined to find something wrong. I was so frustrated, but I couldn't say a thing. I had no control."

"Who else in your life made you feel that way?" I inquired.

"My stepfather!" she cried. "I couldn't please him either. He always found something to yell at me about. Then he would come into my bedroom. I never told anyone. I felt so powerless!"

As she talked, she was able to identify the combination of hurt, fear, and frustration which had led to the overwhelming anger. As we discussed ways to deal with each of those separate feelings, her anger began to subside, and a working plan was made.

Often angry feelings are intensified by similar situations in our past. This is usually the case if the person appears to be more "upset" than is warranted by the situation. Becoming repeatedly upset is a signal that the anger is being fueled by a situation in the past.

Whether the situation and the feelings are a replay of the past or the result of a new occurrence, you can help the person identify the root feeling by listening as the person tells her story and by looking for the fear, hurt, or frustration (or related emotions expressed). Diagram 4.1 illustrates how root feelings are identified.

As the person is telling her story, jot down what she says under the appropriate heading. When she has finished, show her your notes. Ask her if she can recall anything else which has made her feel hurt, fearful, or frustrated. Add these to the list. This will help her to understand why she reacted in anger, put the anger in context, suggesting strategies for dealing with each, as well as showing her where to begin in her struggle to express her anger in a better way.

IDENTIFYING ROOT FEELINGS

Diagram 4.1

Dealing with Hurt

The healing of hurt comes only as we exercise forgiveness, seek restoration (if possible), and experience acceptance. Those from abusive backgrounds have had a lifetime of dealing with hurt. It is not surprising that these people feel as though they have been angry all their lives. In working with someone whose anger arises from hurt, help her see that her anger will not protect against future hurt—it only renders her more vulnerable. Unresolved hurt leads inevitably to bitterness; bitterness is injurious to the spirit.

Forgiveness dissolves anger and restores joy and peace. It may not (and probably will not) change the offending person or the situation, but through forgiveness God can transform the pain inside your friend. You may need to remind your friend that she is to forgive *the person*, not *the wrong act* the person committed. Forgiving means deciding to quit seeking revenge or wanting to punish. Forgiving means agreeing with God to let go of the anger and allowing God to change our hearts. (For more on forgiveness, see chapter 11: "Bitterness.")

Sometimes restoration of the relationship is possible; other times it is neither possible nor wise. This is something you will need to approach after prayer.

Acceptance is the result. Acceptance of the hurt of the past and present situation is the act of forgiveness. Forgiveness is a small emotional price to pay for the insidious pain of continued anger.

Dealing with Frustration

Have you heard it said, "Life is hard, and then you die"? Sometimes, life is just plain hard! The car won't start, the washer breaks down, pipes burst, your child gets sick when you are leaving town, the telephone rings just after you have fallen asleep! Frustration generates anger, because things don't happen as we think they are supposed to happen. We become frustrated when life doesn't play fair! To make it even more frustrating, there is no one to blame! Life *is* just like that sometimes!

The most effective way of helping someone deal with the anger generated by their frustration is to first listen. The simple act of telling another person all that has gone wrong can lead to a new perspective on the frustrations. After you have listened, if your friend is willing, help her problem solve. Is there anything she can do now about the problem? Is there anything she needs someone else to do? When the frustrating incident occurs again, is there anything she can do to make it less aggravating? Making a plan to deal with the immediate problem and being prepared for the next occurrence will do wonders in draining the anger. The energy consumed by the anger becomes channeled into solving the problem.

Sometimes, however, there is no action to take, nothing the person can do. If this is the case, help your friend to verbalize her feelings, then to release the anger and accept the situation as one of those things in life that are just frustrating.

Dealing with Fear

Anger and the accompanying agitation dissipate when fear is faced. We go to great lengths to avoid facing our fears, even when our protective measures cause additional problems!

A man confided, "One of my biggest fears is the fear of being ridiculed. I rarely even think about it, unless I know I'm going to have to speak in public. Then this fear surfaces with a vengeance! I know this fear is not very rational. I have given speeches on numerous occasions. With the exception of one absolutely horrible time, my experiences have been positive. But I still have the fear.

"Recently, I had opportunity to deal with this fear. I didn't do very well. Instead of facing my fear head-on (of being ridiculed), looking at my worst imaginings (everyone in the auditorium hurling insults, jeers, and tomatoes at me), asking God to cleanse me of pride and the need to please everyone (if I didn't please them, they would ridicule me), and preparing my speech (so they wouldn't have a legitimate reason to ridicule me!), I immersed myself in *other* distractions, worries, problems—even creating a few! When was I going to take my cat to the vet? What would I do if . . . ? I became irritable, edgy, and burdened with more than I had begun."

Facing our fears is the only way to receive God's help

and experience His peace. (For more on this subject, see chapter 7: "Fear and Worry.")

Be Angry and Sin Not

Our Father recognized that we would, at times, be angry. We are cautioned to be "slow to anger" (Proverbs 16:32) and to "Let all bitterness and indignation and wrath (passion, rage, bad temper) and resentment (anger, animosity) and quarreling . . . be banished from you" (Ephesians 4:31). How? How can we follow Paul's advice, "When angry, do not sin" (Ephesians 4:26)?

Children whose families required them to deny feelings often grow up believing that expressing emotions is wrong and that feelings are inherently bad. If your friend feels guilty for feeling angry, she will have difficulty understanding the difference between being angry and sinning due to anger.

Since anger can be destructive and result in sin, why did God give us that emotion? The ability to become angry is a gift from God. We can use the energy which anger generates to solve problems.

Mothers Against Drunken Driving (MADD) is a good example of an organization that has used the energy of anger in a constructive way. When those mothers had children killed by drunken drivers, they had choices to make. Would they try to get revenge on the ones who had killed their children? Or would they use that energy to change laws, educate communities, and help to protect the children still alive? Because they made the choice to use their anger constructively, they have been able to be used of God to bring good from the worst kind of tragedies. They have also avoided the bitterness that prolonged anger ensures.

God made us in His image—capable of feeling a wide

variety of emotions, including anger. The Old Testament portrays a God with emotions—including love, grief and sadness over the sins of the people, anger and wrath at disobedience, mercy and understanding, patience and kindness. This capacity to *feel* is part of our inherent God-given nature.

God also created us with liberty or the capacity to make our own choices. When your friend becomes angry, she may not realize she has an opportunity to *choose* how to direct her anger. Because the force of anger is so great, your friend may not realize that she can pause and make a choice before releasing the energy of anger.

When we are hurt, fearful, or frustrated, our first response is to retaliate. We want to get even! To strike back! To make them pay! But retaliation is a destructive choice. When we give in to the temptation to retaliate, whether verbally or physically, we sin. When the "overwhelming flood" (Proverbs 27:4) of anger is released, that flood will produce good or evil, depending upon the choice.

The apostle Paul advised: "Strip yourselves of your former nature [put off and discard your old unrenewed self] which characterized your previous manner of life . . . and put on the new nature (the regenerate self) created in God's image" (Ephesians 4:22, 24).

Our new nature is that part of us which feels and acknowledges the pain, but which chooses to forgive, to face the fear, and to seek solutions. With God's help, we can acknowledge the anger and deal with it constructively.

Ways to Help

Because anger can be such an overwhelming emotion, getting to the root of the anger will not be easy. As you work with others, you may wish to suggest specific steps in working through the anger.

First, encourage her to tell God how she feels. Let your friend know that she doesn't ever need to be afraid to tell God her real feelings. If she has difficulty doing this, suggest that she begin reading the Psalms, noticing how many times David pours out his feelings of hurt, fear, and frustration to God. Remind her that one psalm says to "pour out your hearts before Him," for our Father is "a refuge for us" (Psalm 62:8).

Second, encourage her to give herself time. The old adage of counting to ten is still wise advice. When your friend finds herself becoming angry, encourage her to stop, back off, declare a truce, or call a time out. If she gives herself time to cool down, she will be able to think about dealing with the problem in a godly manner.

"A goal of yours should be to help your friend find ways to express her anger which hurt neither herself nor others. She has to vent her angry feelings without feeling condemned."

Third, do something physical. Because it is difficult to deal with the root problems at the height of the anger, some of that excess energy may need to be worked off before your friend is ready to mentally tackle the problem. Suggest that she mop the floor, take a walk, clean out a closet or storeroom, or play baseketball—anything physical!

Fourth, do not procrastinate. Help your friend to set a time to deal with the problem. She can count to ten, do something physical, and give herself time to get over the initial fury, but she doesn't need to put off solving the problem! The Bible advises us not to let our fury last until the sun goes down (Ephesians 4:26). An unsolved problem doesn't go away. It just becomes bigger and bigger.

Fifth, advise her not to spend time with the "what if's" or the "if only's." If your friend has made a mistake, she must not waste her mental or physical energy berating herself or wishing she could change things. This is only a diversion of Satan to keep her from actually confronting the problem and solving it.

Sixth, help her to resolve to see it through and to make a plan for next time. Help your friend use the situation to allow God to demonstrate His faithfulness to her. Let Him use it to teach her new skills and to prepare her with a "plan of action" should a similar situation arise. Make each experience count. Don't waste failures. Let God use them to teach her and to heal her. Each time your friend *and God* work through an experience of anger together, her new habits are strengthened. She will learn new things. She will be free!

Acceptance

In working with those who are angry, remember that many don't know how to deal with their feelings in an appropriate manner. A goal of yours should be to help your friend find ways to express her anger which hurts neither herself nor others. She has to vent her angry feelings without feeling condemned.

STEPS TOWARD RESOLUTION

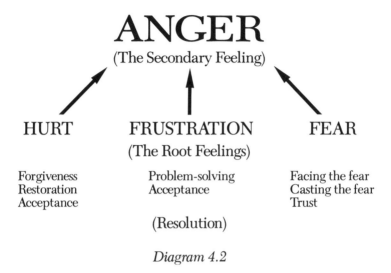

ANGER
(The Secondary Feeling)

HURT   FRUSTRATION   FEAR

(The Root Feelings)

Forgiveness	Problem-solving	Facing the fear
Restoration	Acceptance	Casting the fear
Acceptance		Trust

(Resolution)

Diagram 4.2

It may help to draw up a written contract with one who has been violent or self-destructive in the past. In that agreement, she promises neither to hurt herself or another nor do anything which could potentially hurt herself or another (for example, driving a car too fast when angry).

After you have established ways to handle the initial surge of energy, begin teaching your friend to identify the root feeling. Keeping a diagram of the steps, such as diagram 4.2 above, is a helpful reminder of how to deal with each root problem.

As she gets practice in dealing with hurt, fear, and frustration, no longer will her anger seem so overwhelming and frightening. She will have learned to acknowledge her anger—and deal with it. This is no small achievement. You will have given her tools she will be able to use for a lifetime.

LIFE APPLICATIONS ─────────────────

1. What do people do that makes you the most angry?

2. How does your body act out your anger?

3. Can you recall a time when you became angry, lost control, and sinned? What did you do, and what was the result? Can you identify the root cause?

4. Share a time in which you have chosen to get revenge. What was the result? Did you have peace?

5. Are you surprised when life becomes extremely difficult? Do you feel imposed upon? Are you frequently frustrated?

6. Are you usually able to find more than one direction to focus the energy that comes with your anger?

7. Can you recall a time when you have been angry, confronted the one who provoked you, solved the problem, and honored God?

8. What are some ways to help a friend who is angry?

7

FEAR AND WORRY

Anxiety in a man's heart weighs it down. . . .
PROVERBS 12:25

Anxiety, the fruit of fear and worry, is one of the most common complaints of those seeking counsel. Throughout the Old and New Testaments, we are cautioned about the effects of fear and worry. We are instructed not to be fearful or to worry. Nevertheless, we can easily succumb to anxiety.

In the summer of 1990, an earthquake was predicted to occur in December along the New Madrid fault line which lies in northeast Arkansas and southeast Missouri. My husband, Wayne, was working at a new job, only twenty miles from the fault line. At first, I didn't really pay much attention to the media's doomsday predictions. Some said the death toll would number in the thousands, and the damage would extend over several states, with collapsed buildings and bridges, power failures, and extensive flooding along the banks of the Mississippi River, yet I managed to stay calm.

I became "concerned," however, as I, too, was swept up by the reactions of people around me. Many in central Arkansas were purchasing earthquake insurance and stocking up on water, food, and other supplies. Communities within the predicted disaster area were staging earthquake drills, packing away their valuables, canceling schools, and making plans to leave the area the first week of December.

In spite of the reassurances of respected geologists who said an earthquake would probably not occur during that specific time period, and in the light of others who claimed they had no fear and who had even hired bands to play for "Shake, Rattle, and Roll" parties, *my* imagination began to take over, and I began to play disaster scenes in my mind. What if something happened to Wayne? What if the earthquake occurred and telephone lines were down? How could I find out if he was all right? What if collapsed bridges made it impossible for me to get to him? If only I could persuade him to take a few days off during that dreaded week in December!

My fear was compounded by frustration when Wayne completely resisted my efforts to impress him with the potential danger he faced! He refused to take vacation days that week and told me his employer had already taken precautions to ensure his safety. He didn't even believe the earthquake would occur! (By this time, of course, I was convinced of the worst case scenarios created by the media.) I could not understand how Wayne could go about his work unperturbed and optimistic. Didn't he understand? Didn't he care how I felt? My heart became weighted down as my anxiety grew (Proverbs 12:25).

The Roots of Fear and Worry

Why do we worry about what may happen—or what *did* happen—or what *might not* happen? Why do we long to know *now* what will happen later or fret about things which have already occurred? As you counsel friends, you will find fear and worry to be common, even among those in the body of Christ.

"Fear and worry flow from particular beliefs or expectations about life. Many of the things we believe simply are not true."

Christians are not immune to fear and worry, despite instructions to "stop being perpetually uneasy (anxious and worried) about your life . . ." (Matthew 6:25) and to cast "the whole of your care [all your anxieties, all your worries, all your concerns once and for all] on Him . . ." (1 Peter 5:7).

To help those bound by fear and worry, we need an understanding of how people, even Christians, get caught in fear and worry.

The Fear and Worry Habit

For some, fear and worry are simply habits, which are usually learned from other family members.

Ask your friend some preliminary questions: Is there someone in her family who is fearful? Is there a worrier?

Were her parents overly protective? Did she hear the insistent "Be careful" and "Don't try that. You might get hurt" warnings as she was growing up?

Was she encouraged to try ideas and skills on her own, or were things done for her? When parents do things for a child that she can do for herself, the child grows up feeling inadequate, incompetent, and afraid to attempt new things.

Others resort to the habit of fear and worry as a way to relieve boredom. Some people use worry as they would a drug, to add intensity to their lives, to add color and excitement to certain situations. A woman waiting in line to board a plane said, "This is my first flight! Did you read about the big crash in Denver last week? Oh, I just hope we make it!" Intensity and drama made her feel alive. Unfortunately, she had learned to rely upon fear and worry to make her life exciting.

The Fear and Worry Lies

Fear and worry flow from particular beliefs or expectations about life. Many of the things we believe simply are not true. Does the person with whom you are working believe any of the following lies which feed fear and worry?

"God won't help me." Even though our Father reassures us of His knowledge of our situation, His intention, as well as His ability to help us, many continue to worry and to be afraid. You may want to ask your friend if she believes that God *will* take care of her. Does she believe God *does* care? Has God helped her in the past? How? Why would God not help her now?

"I can't do it." Fear paralyzes. When a person is fearful, she may believe she is incapable of taking any kind of action or changing her thinking. For some, this sort of reasoning

has become habitual. For others, the fear prevents them from facing the problem and beginning to resolve it.

"I wouldn't worry about you if I didn't love you." Many believe that worry communicates love. This is particularly true between parents and children. For example, have you ever heard, "Of course, I worry about you! I'm your mother. I love you!" However, the opposite is true. When you tell a person you are worried about her, you often actually send a clear message that you don't think she is capable. Worry and love are not the same. Worry and concern are not the same. Worry words do not produce the peace that love brings; they only introduce anxiety.

"If I worry enough about this possible catastrophe, maybe it won't happen!" Worry will never magically prevent catastrophe. Does the person with whom you are working believe worry will keep things from happening or protect her? Unfortunately, the opposite is often true; worry paralyzes us with fear, preventing us from taking the steps to face, plan for, or stop the feared event from occurring.

Lucille was aware that her company had planned layoffs for her department. She related, "I was so worried! What if I were let go? What would I do? How would I support myself and my children? I couldn't sleep at night worrying about my job!

"When the layoff was announced, my worst fears came true. I had been let go! No matter how much I worried, it didn't make any difference. In fact, my boss told me he had hated to let me go, but over the last months my performance had deteriorated because I had been so preoccupied!"

"If I am worrying, at least I'm doing something about

the problem!" Worry makes us feel as if we are doing something, even though we are not. It provides a false sense of progress.

Worry is not the same as planning or taking constructive action in thought or results. Planning is an action that seeks God's guidance in finding specific, creative steps to solve a problem. On the other hand, worry simply produces confusion.

Worry as Avoidance

Some use worry about one problem to avoid facing another one. When a person is afraid she will be overwhelmed by one problem, she may decide to worry about another problem that may not be as threatening.

For example, Janis was a young woman who requested counseling for a weight problem. After several sessions, she said, "I realize that when my husband and I began to have marriage problems, I began to worry about my weight. I began several diets, but I couldn't stick to any of them. I thought about my weight constantly, but I never did anything constructive about it. I see now that I wasn't really concerned about my weight but was avoiding the fact that my marriage was in serious trouble. I was afraid that if I did face the problems in my marriage, I would become unglued!"

When a person uses worry as a distraction, she is creating additional problems. Avoiding a problem by becoming fearful or worried about something else only allows the problem to multiply.

A Spirit of Fear

Scripture clearly teaches, "For God did not give us a spirit of timidity (of cowardice, of craven and cringing and fawning fear), but [He has given us a spirit] of power and of love and of calm and well-balanced mind and discipline and self-control" (2 Timothy 1:7). A spirit of fear comes from Satan, whose main purpose is to kill, steal, and destroy (see John 10:10). A spirit of fear prevents us from experiencing the power, love, and peace that God gives to all His children. As you counsel, be aware that the battle is not only in the mind but also in the spiritual realm.

If a person is fearful, for seemingly no reason, it is likely that a spirit of fear is involved. A person under attack by Satan doesn't understand why she is feeling the way she is, why she feels as if she has no control.

If you sense your friend is under the influence of a spirit of fear, ask God for discernment. Talk to a mature Christian or your pastor who has experience in spiritual warfare. Pray for guidance. If your impression continues to be confirmed, ask your friend if you can pray with her about any spirits of fear that may be present.

Remember that the name of Jesus is the Name above all names and that "in (at) the name of Jesus every knee should (must) bow, in heaven and on earth and under the earth" (Philippians 2:10). When you pray for your friend in the name of Jesus, pray that all spirits not of God will be prevented from harassing the person. (For further information on spiritual warfare, see chapter 17.)

Ways to Help

After examining with your friend the roots of her fear and anger, you are ready to lead her in the steps to healing in this area.

Surrender

First, talk with your friend about entrusting herself to God's will. The quickest way to have peace of mind is to let God have His way, believing that His way is best.

Is she willing to put aside her fear or worry? Is she willing to *entrust* herself to God? Fear and worry are choices. Is she willing to choose another way?

Can she wholeheartedly agree with David and say, "But I trusted in, relied on, and was confident in You, O Lord; I said, You are my God. My times are in Your hands" (Psalm 31:14–15)?

Confess the Sin of Fear and Worry

Ask your friend to confess fear and worry as the sins that they are.

As I continued to allow the predictions of the earthquake to consume me, my fears multiplied. The problem became magnified. I was extra sensitive to anything connected to earthquake stories. Finally, I realized I had focused on myself and my own thoughts concerning this potential problem instead of on God and His protection. In doing so, I had grieved the Holy Spirit. I confessed my worry as a sin and asked God for His forgiveness and help.

Identify the Root Problem

Identifying the root problem will help you know where to begin. Is it a matter of breaking old habits? Of choosing to trust and not to worry? If your friend is having problems with trust, help her to remember God's faithfulness to her in the past. Try to identify another time when she was afraid or worried. What was the outcome? How did God help, rescue, guide, or direct her?

Is the problem due to believing one or more of these lies about fear and worry? Is she using worry to avoid dealing with a particular problem? Does there seem to be a spirit of fear operating?

Face the Fear

Help your friend to be as specific as possible as she defines the situation, fear, worry, or problem. If there are several areas of concern, pray with your friend for guidance concerning which area to approach first. This will relieve any feeling of being overwhelmed and will provide a starting place.

A fear that is faced is a fear on the way to extinction. Usually, when we finally face the root of fear or worry, it is not nearly so awful or as big as we thought.

Make a Plan

What is the worst thing that can happen? What would she do if that did occur? Making a plan to deal with the possible worries will lessen the intensity of the fear or worry.

First, pray for answers. As soon as a problem occurs, encourage your friend to seek God's guidance. It is important that His guidance is followed promptly. Prompt action is a good deterrent to worry. Obeying God will bring relief and strengthen her against the temptation to worry.

Second, ask the person what she has already done. If she has taken some productive steps, recognize them and use them to encourage her to further trust and obey.

Third, ask if there is anything which God has led her to do that she has not done. If there is, encourage her to obey God. Other guidance will probably not come until obedience follows guidance which He has already given. Help her focus on what she can do rather than on what she cannot do.

Fourth, make a list of things she can do that she has not done. Help her to set a time when she will do the things she can do.

Fifth, fill the mind with God's thoughts. Encourage your friend to write down Scripture verses and place them in a prominent place. Ask her to say them aloud frequently. This will help to transfer thoughts of worry into thoughts of faith.

God led me to memorize Psalm 121. As I wrote out that psalm and repeated it several times daily, the fear within me began to dissolve. Paul said that God's Word is "alive and full of power" (Hebrews 4:12). As His Word became imprinted in my mind, my fear was overcome by His power.

Encourage your friend to substitute her thoughts of fear and worry with God's Word. We are told to "lead every thought and purpose away captive into the obedience of Christ" (2 Corinthians 10:5). When she is tempted to worry, to imagine what might happen, or to become fearful, encourage her to drive away her imaginations with the Word of God. God's Word will sanctify a harmful imagination.

You might want to suggest that she do a Scripture study on the phrase "fear not," and write out reasons Scripture gives for not fearing. Or she could write out and personalize specific scriptural passages dealing with her problem. Examples are Isaiah 27:3–4; Deuteronomy 31:8; 2 Timothy 1:7; Psalms 23, 25, 103, 121; Proverbs 3:5–8; Matthew 6:25–34; Philippians 4:6–9; and Hebrews 13:5.

Sixth, continually give thanks. In the midst of a crisis, it is easy to overlook the good things God does. A thankful heart is a lighter heart. Encourage your friend to give thanks and praise to God as He works on her behalf.

Seventh, find comfort while waiting. If God doesn't guide your friend into action immediately, encourage her to be willing to wait until He does. The temptation to worry can be very difficult for some people and can lead them to fabricate their own answers. It helps to set aside a definite time each day to pray and to listen for God's instructions.

Worry causes us to lose sight of the needs of others. Often, God allows us to help others while we wait on Him. We are promised that when we give, God will return it to us, shaken down, pressed together, and running over (Luke 6:38).

My fears and worries about an earthquake had so narrowed my perspective that I thought only of my own husband and no one else. God instructed me to begin to pray diligently, not only for Wayne, but also for all people who were in possible danger.

One weekend in late November, I drove up the fault line to visit Wayne. As I passed exit signs for various small towns, I prayed aloud for each one. As I prayed, I realized I was no longer afraid of danger. When I arrived in the town where Wayne was working, I drove up and down various streets, praying that God's safety would prevail and His Spirit would move among the people there.

By turning my mind to the needs of others, and bringing their needs before God, He freed me from my own fears and worries!

And finally, get information on the subject. Find out what your friend knows about her problem. Sometimes ignorance increases worry that basic information could alleviate.

After All Else Has Been Done, Cast the Care

The Bible tells us to cast the whole of our cares, anxieties, worries and concerns, once and for all, on God, because He cares for us affectionately and watchfully (1 Peter 5:7).

"When she is tempted to worry, to imagine what might happen, or to become fearful, encourage her to drive away her imaginations with the Word of God. God's Word will sanctify a harmful imagination."

What Is a Care?

A care is the emotional burden we carry concerning a problem. It is the *feeling that accompanies* worry. After your friend has entrusted her fear or worry to God and has done all that God leads her to do, care is the remaining heavy weight within us. God tells us to cast it off onto Him.

How to Cast a Care

Casting a care is a spiritual transaction, like forgiveness or salvation. Although it is something that we decide to do, it is actually accomplished by God, because we can't do it for ourselves. When we choose to cast the care, God does on the inside of us what we can't do for ourselves.

Help your friend to *do* something that will signify her part of this spiritual transaction. One way is to ask your friend to write down all her anxieties, fears, and worries on pieces of paper and to place these in a box. Next, take twine and tie the box together with lots of knots. Put the box where it can be seen often, that can represent an altar. Seeing the box on the "altar" will be a constant reminder of her release to God to do His work on her behalf.

There are many variations on this theme. One woman said she put her cares in a shoe box, tied it tightly, drove to the dumpster in her apartment complex, and tossed it over. Another woman placed her list in her kitchen sink, set fire to it, and offered her cares to God as they became ashes.

Whatever she chooses to do, the action will make a mental impression that symbolizes her spiritual transaction with God and guards against her taking the cares up again.

The date for the earthquake came and went. The earthquake did not happen—all my fears and worries had been for nothing. Yet God used my fears and worries to again teach me of His power, His love, and His perfect peace. He led me through my crisis of fear, and made His Word real to me:

> You will guard him and keep him in perfect and constant peace whose mind [both its inclination and its character] is stayed on You, because he commits himself to You, leans on You, and hopes confidently in You.
>
> So trust in the Lord (commit yourself to Him, lean on Him, hope confidently in Him) forever; for the Lord God is an everlasting Rock [the Rock of Ages]. (Isaiah 26:3–4)

LIFE APPLICATIONS

1. What is your greatest fear?

2. Did your parents encourage you to meet chal-

lenges, or were they overly protective? Give an example, and tell how your experience affected you.

3. Have you ever equated love and worry? How? Have your parents, mates, or friends done this? How?

4. What is your "favorite worry"? How do you use it to distract yourself from more serious matters?

5. Can you share a time when you became fearful and could not regain control without the help of a friend?

6. Have you ever used the Name of Jesus to fight fears?

7. Share a time when you have faced a fear. How did you feel afterward?

8. Have you ever experienced a fear due to lack of information? Give an example. What difference did the information make?

9. What are some ways you can help a friend who is fearful?

10. Optional Exercise: Write on separate pieces of paper any anxieties, fears, or worries. Place these in a box. Tie the box together with twine, string, or ribbon, making many knots. Place the box where it can be seen often, as if on an altar. Use it is a reminder that you have released your concerns and cares to God. Memorize 1 Peter 5:7.

8

GRIEF

For my heart was grieved, embittered, and in a state
of ferment, and I was pricked in my heart. . . .
PSALM 73:21

"Why, God? Why Mary? Why did she have to die? She had a husband and two little children! Why, God, why?"

The anguish was evident in Lily's voice as she told me of watching her childhood friend take her last breath. "One minute Mary was there, weak but alive. The next minute as I stood watching, my childhood friend was gone, dead at age twenty-eight from leukemia.

"Mary had her life in good order. My years of teenage rebellion extended into my twenties, but Mary had settled down, married, become a nurse, and had two beautiful children. When she came to know God in a very close way and tried to share her new experiences with me, I didn't want to listen. Now she was gone.

"Walking out of the hospital, I felt numb. I couldn't believe the sun was still shining, that life went on. Anger flooded my heart. I wanted to cry, to lash out. I was angry at the smiling people who were looking forward to visits with loved ones. Everything felt unreal and suspended. I felt drained and energized at the same time. As the psalmist, I felt grieved, embittered, in a state of ferment, and pricked in my heart (Psalm 73:21)!"

While death is certainly one of the most grievous losses a person will experience, as you counsel others you will find many situations where grief is part of the process. Most changes, whether desired or undesired, involve some type of loss and, as a result, a certain amount of grief. How can you help a person who is grieving?

What Is Grief?

Grief is an overwhelming feeling of sorrow, pain, regret, and sadness. We feel as if our heart is broken—that nothing will ever be the same—that happiness will never be possible again.

Grief is actual loss, as well as the feelings associated with that loss. A part of us is missing; we are unsettled—flooded with regrets for what cannot be.

We have all experienced losses. Which of the following have you or someone you know experienced within the last two years?

- death of a close relative or friend

- divorce

- a move

- break-up of a relationship

- job change

- church change

- loss of a job

112

- health problems
- death of a pet
- loss of personal possessions
- loss of property
- loss of position
- financial setback
- child leaving home
- marriage of a friend or child
- moving away of a friend or child
- a lost opportunity

You have probably experienced many other losses, both positive and negative. Some losses are forced on us, and some we choose. Even when the loss is chosen, some degree of grief is often experienced. Usually, "losses" which are forced upon us are the most difficult to accept, especially if they are losses we would not have chosen.

"Grief is an overwhelming feeling of sorrow, pain, regret, and sadness."

Joyce, a young woman in her thirties, had first come to counseling several years ago, following the death of her young husband from AIDS. Now, five years later, she was back in the office, facing another great loss. Over the previous year, she herself had been hospitalized twice for extended periods due to complications from AIDS which she had contracted from her husband. Weak but determined after her last bout with illness, she said, "Facing the fact that I may die is hard enough; I don't want to die *now*. But what seems hardest right now is dealing with all the things I have no control over—my strength, my medical treatment, all the unknowns! I didn't choose this illness—and I feel that I have few choices about anything in my life!" Joyce was confronted with a number of losses, none of which she wanted or had chosen.

As you work with those who are experiencing grief, you will need to reassure them that their feelings are normal. Often people hesitate to share their feelings, because they are afraid of sounding weird or crazy. Assure them that *grief is a process, and their feelings are normal.*

The Stages of Grief

Although the process of grief has several stages, predictable emotions are unique to each stage. Everyone will not experience or react in the same way, but being aware of some of the most frequently reported feelings will help you counsel friends who experience grief.

Shock—The Emotional Shut-Off Valve

The first emotion most people experience is shock—a numbness or a feeling of unreality.

"Standing there in the room with Mary that last day, I knew she was gone," Lily continued. "Yet as I walked out of the hospital room, I felt like an actor in a play. In just a minute, Mary would get out of the bed, we would take a break, and then replay the scene again. My mind was unable to accept that I wouldn't be coming back to visit

Mary—that I wouldn't see her anymore—that she was truly dead."

This initial numbness is God's anesthesia, His way of protecting us for a time. All of our emotional systems shut off for a period, in order to help us absorb the initial shock and to give us time to begin to adjust. During this time, a grieving person may act normally and seem to be without feeling. She may carry on the details of her life with unusual calmness and composure. However, all too soon, the numbness wears off.

Anger and Anxiety—The Feeling Fruit Basket

Lily related to me her mixed feelings at the funeral service. "How can the sun still be shining? How can these people act as if nothing is wrong? I wanted to stand up and yell at them. I wanted to grab someone and just shake them. I wanted to burst into tears.

"I should have told her how much she meant to me. I should have told her I was sorry for not seeing her more. I should have . . ." the thoughts went on and on.

"During the funeral, my thoughts turned to my own death. What if *I* died now? Would I have left anything of value? Would I be missed?" Anger and guilt turned quickly into worry and fear. Then quickly back to guilt. "Here I am thinking about myself when I should be thinking about Mary's family!" Then, "Why did she have to die? I just don't understand!"

From the state of feeling nothing, we enter into a hodgepodge of feelings. We feel anger and fear. We worry. We feel guilt. We are gripped by one powerful emotion after another. It is as though the heart and mind compensate for the period of numbness by overwhelming us with new and intense emotions.

When it becomes too painful to feel the hurt, the grieving person gets mad instead. She blames, rails out at God, other people, and even herself. During this time, she may berate herself for the things she didn't do. She may become angry at the person who died, divorced her, or left her. She may also be angry at God for allowing the event to occur.

This stage can be very frightening to those who have been taught that anger is wrong or to those who don't know how to deal with anger. (For further information on this subject, see chapter 6: "Anger.") Fear and anxiety fuel this anger. Questions like, "What will I do now?" "How can I go on?" "What will happen to the children?" "How can I manage without this person, job, situation?" will repeat themselves incessantly in the mind of the grieving person.

The unknown is very frightening for most of us. Feeling as though we have some measure of control makes us feel more secure. When facing the unknown, there are no common footholds, no knowledge of what skills will be needed. Nothing is predictable!

During this stage of anger and anxiety, the most important thing you can do is let your grieving friend know that you are with her and that you will continue to be with her during this confusing time. Your presence is worth more than anything else.

Depression—The Transition

None of us can operate at peak intensity for long. In between and following the high intensity emotions of anger and anxiety, most people pass through a transition stage in which the predominant feeling is depression.

During the months after Mary's death, it seemed that every time Lily turned around, there was something to remind her of Mary. A song, girls giggling, running into an old Sunday school teacher—she would find herself with tears coming to her eyes at the most unexpected moments.

She didn't seem to have very much energy. Just as she would think she was feeling "normal," something would happen to remind Lily that *Mary was gone*. Then, she would feel bad for feeling happy, and the tears would come again.

Often, depression is anger turned inward. The anger may be toward someone else or toward oneself. Guilt is one of the most common emotions that fuels anger toward oneself. "Why didn't I . . . ? Why did I . . . ? If only I had. . . ." But guilt has a double whammy: it comes when the bereaved person forgets her grief, if only for a moment. She will find herself laughing, enjoying a meal, or just relaxing. As you counsel with a grieving person, be aware that this false guilt is normal and that part of her depression at this stage may, in fact, be anger at herself.

Usually, a grieving person will vacillate between the "feeling fruit basket" and depression. These often completely opposite feelings may be experienced in full within the same hour! During the depression stage, the grieving person may not want to go anywhere, see others, or engage in her normal activities. She may want to simply talk and think about the person she has lost. Again, the most important thing you can do for your friend is to be with her, listen, and offer your support.

Acceptance—The Beginning of Healing

"As I marked the first anniversary of Mary's death on my calendar, I felt a combination of feelings," Lily related. "The pain of the loss lingered, but it was different. I thought of things about the past year I would like to have shared with her—my decision to follow Jesus and the beginning of so many of the changes in my life that we had discussed. I found comfort knowing that she was in heaven and that somehow she knew. Although I still missed her, I realized that I had said good-bye."

Acceptance does not mean that the person or situation wasn't important or loved or isn't still missed. Sometimes a grieving person equates acceptance with dismissal.

Acceptance means that you have quit living in the past, as though the person were still a part of your life, and that you have decided to begin a new chapter of your life. You don't forget the person. You don't dismiss the feelings you had. You simply choose to go on with your life.

The Importance of Grieving

By attempting to detour around the grief process and go immediately to the "acceptance" phase, some think they can bypass the pain. Unfortunately, grief doesn't work this way. A grieving person must allow herself to face and experience her grief in order to begin the journey toward healing.

Many fear the grieving process because of the intense and uncomfortable nature of its emotions. We think that if we don't "feel the feelings," somehow they will magically go away. We fear that we will be completely overwhelmed. Others may be afraid to show emotions, believing it is a sign of weakness. Therefore, feelings are denied.

Denial only works for a time and is a false comfort. Grief is necessary. It is necessary because without the expression of the grief there is no comfort. Jesus said, "Blessed . . . are those who mourn, for they shall be comforted!" (Matthew 5:4). If we deny or delay our feelings, we deny and delay our healing.

In the story of Joseph, we are given a picture of a man who was willing to face the painful emotion of grief. In his youth, Joseph had been sold as a slave to Egypt. The Bible describes him as being a handsome young man as well as an intelligent, capable one. So highly regarded was he that his power eventually was second only to Pharaoh's over the whole of Egypt. Joseph was a man with whom to reckon!

Yet, when Joseph's father, Jacob, died, Joseph "fell upon his father's face and wept over him and kissed him," and Joseph wept and bemoaned his father for seventy days (Genesis 50:1–3). Following this seventy-day period of mourning, Jacob was buried, and there was another seven-day period in which Joseph and his household "mourned with a great lamentation and extreme demonstrations of sorrow" (Genesis 50:10).

Joseph knew the importance of the grieving process. He didn't rush himself, nor did he deny his feelings. As you work with a person who is grieving, assure her that grieving is necessary. It is the prerequisite to healing. Give her "permission" to grieve and don't try to rush her through it. Each person has her own pace. Your part is to be with her in any way that you can.

The Importance of Ceremonies

In Joseph's day, there was a fixed number of days for the embalming process and for the periods of lamentations and mournings. The importance of endings and of saying good-bye was understood. A formalized time for saying good-bye aids greatly in beginning again. This is true not only in the major endings, such as death, but also in smaller, almost insignificant endings.

"On our daughter Sara's fourth birthday," Laura related, "our old cat died. He was a gentle animal who loved to play with Sara and sit in her lap. He followed her from room to room and even out in the yard, as if to keep an eye on her. Sara had great difficulty saying goodbye to her animal pal.

"So, instead of letting our vet dispose of the cat's body,

we took him home. Sara chose one of her cotton baby blankets to wrap him in, and we placed the cat on a doll pillow in a small cardboard box. Sara kept one of his toys as a memento, and placed the rest of them in the box. Then, we all went out together and buried him under the apple tree.

"Our daughter is six now. She still mentions her cat once in a while, usually to tell a funny story. Participating in his 'funeral' helped Sara separate from her pet."

Since Laura told me this, I have repeatedly seen the importance of ceremonies. A ceremony serves as closure on a situation or relationship. It provides a concrete reminder of a formal good-bye. It helps in the transition process.

Ceremonies are important, whether the ceremony is a memorial service, the simple burial of a loved animal, a graduation, a commemoration of an act of forgiveness, a transaction of some kind, a dedication, or retirement. It provides a signpost, a memorial, a specific time for saying good-bye.

When Grief Becomes Unhealthy

The Bible says that there is "a time to weep and a time to laugh, a time to mourn and a time to dance" (Ecclesiastes 3:4). There is no set time for a person to grieve. Some people may need to grieve for longer periods than others. The time necessary for grieving will depend upon the person, the type of loss, as well as a host of other variables. However, there are some warning signs, or indicators, that the person may be entering into a stage of "unhealthy" grief.

The Bondage of Mourning

The mistaken idea that the intensity and length of the grief are directly related to the love one had for the person (or job or situation) is not uncommon.

The following exchange was overheard between two women in the aisle of a grocery store:

"Why, I heard that John Brown is getting ready to marry some woman he grew up with. And poor Mary hardly cold in her grave! Can you believe it?"

"No! And I always thought John and Mary had such a good marriage. You just never can tell these days, can you?"

Somehow we believe that if a person quits her outward show of grief and gets on with her life before a certain, unspecified length of time has passed, she didn't really love the person who left. Often the grieving person will hesitate to begin new things just because others have this expectation, even though she doesn't feel it herself.

Feeling guilty for desiring to move ahead or thinking this may signify she didn't really care is unhealthy grief. It is a denial of grief in reverse, a denial of the healing God has begun in that person.

Don't force a person to move beyond the point where she is able, but neither discourage a person from moving ahead as she expresses the desire. Each person will know when she is free to date again, enjoy herself, or begin something new. Many don't because of what others may think. Starting over doesn't negate the positive feelings of the past. It simply means that the healing process has begun.

The Ways to Recognition

"But if I quit grieving, people will forget about me! I never realized that people cared about me until my son's tragic death."

As strange as it may seem, some people hold on to their grief in an attempt to feel important. The tragic event and their subsequent grief are, to them, the only way to receive recognition. Because of their loss, others take notice of them. They are important. People care. Giving up the grief means giving up the attention.

This prolonged type of grief is unhealthy because it forces a person to remain fixed in the past. It forces her to relive the past—the events, the feelings, the pain—to enjoy the limelight of center stage. What is sad is the person doesn't learn healthy ways to satisfy her need for attention and recognition. She remains a victim of her trauma.

The Poor-Me Rut

When any tragedy occurs—whether death, divorce, or the loss of a job—we naturally feel compassion and sorrow for the one going through the difficulty. Some who grieve, however, begin to revel in their role as the afflicted and use their pain to manipulate others. One woman told me her story, saying:

> I was shocked and heartbroken when my brother-in-law left my sister. She had a new baby and a three-year-old. I felt so sorry for her. She didn't know many people, and I worried about her all the time. My husband and I tried to help her out in every way we could. I cooked and baby-sat for her. My husband mowed her yard and helped her straighten out her bills. We even got a lawyer friend of ours to give her free counsel. But it's been over a year now. She is still very angry with her ex-husband; she still expects us to take care of her affairs. I have three kids of my own. I don't know how much longer we are going to be able to help her!

When a person begins to see herself as a victim because of the situation and begins to expect others to do things for her, her grief may actually be self-pity.

Self-pity is not healthy and, in fact, is a sin. Self-pity both denies and negates God's healing power. When a person indulges in self-pity, she will tend to magnify what is wrong in her life, giving little recognition to the good. She becomes wrapped up in herself, focusing on the pain and ignoring God's provision and comfort.

It is difficult to help a person who is engulfed in self-pity because, often, the person is receiving secondary gains. When this is the case, the person is hesitant to give these up and assume control of her life.

When the person you are trying to help resists looking at her blessings, engages in self-indulgent behaviors using her grief as an excuse, refuses to handle things herself, or becomes angry when you make suggestions, the natural grief may have degenerated into unhealthy self-pity.

A Spirit of Grief

A fourth form of unhealthy grief needs to be mentioned— that of satanic attack. When the Christian entertains the accusations of the father of lies about God's goodness, love, and kind intentions, she becomes bound by grief. Satan is the master deceiver, and his goal is to lie, kill, steal, and destroy (John 10:10). Satan will attempt to prevent a person from experiencing the comfort and love of God as she moves through the grieving process. He will attempt to keep her from receiving God's healing and strength. Most of us are very vulnerable spiritually during a time of grief and change. Satan may attack us; and if we aren't aware of his strategies, we won't know why we feel oppressed.

One difference between a normal, healthy grieving process and a spirit of grief sent by Satan centers around control. A person who is being attacked by Satan doesn't understand why she has no control over her feelings. She feels blocked from receiving God's comfort, although she knows the comfort is hers for the asking. It is as though she isn't in charge of her feelings. She may, in fact, express feelings she has never had before, which are inconsistent with her personality, such as thoughts of suicide. She usually feels hopeless and somewhat lethargic—more so than one would feel normally when grieving.

If you sense your friend may be under the attack of Satan, ask God for discernment. Talk to someone who has experience in spiritual warfare. Pray for guidance. If your impression continues to be confirmed, ask the person if you can pray with her about satanic attack and oppression.

Remember that the name of Jesus is the Name above all names and that "in (at) the name of Jesus every knee should (must) bow, in heaven and on earth and under the earth" (Philippians 2:10). When you pray for the person in the name of Jesus, pray that the accuser and adversary, which is what "Satan" means in Hebrew, will be prevented from harassing her. (For further information on spiritual warfare, see chapter 17.)

Ways to Help

As with other areas of personal struggle, you can help your friend through your counseling in a number of ways.

Be There

Many people are uncomfortable around someone who is grieving because they don't know what to say. Instead of respecting silences and simply sitting with them, often we simply avoid the grieving person altogether.

During the initial phases of grief, the person doesn't need our conversation. Her mind is still in shock; she is unable to think clearly. Thinking is too painful. All her energy is consumed with coping. There is little energy left to process a lot of well-meaning words from people.

"Never underestimate the power of your presence with someone in their time of grief."

During times of grief, most people don't remember the words you say to them. They do remember you were there. One woman told me, "When my grandmother died some years ago, I hadn't known my friend Janis very long. So I was surprised when I saw her at the funeral. She hadn't known my grandmother, and she barely knew me. Yet she cared enough to take time from work and to come to the funeral. Her presence there spoke volumes to me. I felt that Jesus had sent her there especially for me. I was deeply touched by her gesture. I felt loved and comforted."

Never underestimate the power of your presence with someone in their time of grief. Be there. You will never know how much that will mean to them.

Fill a Need

Many times, the grieving person does not know what she needs until that need is filled. Don't just offer your services. Serve. Do something.

When Kathy's husband left her and her two young sons, she was devastated. She didn't have a good relationship with her parents, and keeping up with her active youngsters left little time for making friends. She had never felt so alone in her life, nor so overwhelmed. In describing that terrible time in her life, she spoke of her gratitude.

> I couldn't have made it had it not been for my next-door neighbor, Sue. It was uncanny. Just when I thought I would reach my breaking point, Sue would show up at my door. Sometimes she would come over to take the boys to the park; other times she came by on the way to the grocery store, always managing to get a list of my grocery needs to buy them for me. She brought over pound cake and made coffee, just sitting at my kitchen table ready to listen. Little things. Big things. If Sue hadn't been there for me, I don't think I would have made it.

Ask God to show you what you can do to help the person who is grieving. Think of the little, everyday things. Don't offer. Many people are hesitant to ask for help, and a person who is grieving is less likely to even know what she needs! If you say, "Call me if there's anything I can do," you probably will not be called. Ask God to give you the opportunity to fill a need.

Listen

If the grieving person wants to talk, listen. This is not the time to deliver discourses on faith, the purpose of pain, suffering, or other theological issues. Just listen.

Share Your Memories

Many times it is helpful for the grieving person to reminisce with others about the one she has lost. This is especially true when the loss is one of death. If the person wants to talk about her loved one, share a memory of that person with her. Talk about how you first met him, the influence he had on your life, funny things you remember, times you shared. It is a comfort to know that other people enjoyed being with the one you have lost and that he was important to them.

Look at pictures of the person. This is especially helpful for children who have lost a parent, grandparent, close friend, or family member. Encourage your friend to reminisce if she wants to do so.

Use God's Word to Comfort

God is described as the source of every comfort, consolation and encouragement (2 Corinthians 1:3). His Word is alive and active, full of power, with the ability to energize and to comfort in any situation (Hebrews 4:12). When the grieving person seems receptive, remind her of God's love, His care, and His comfort. Be sensitive to the leading of the Spirit, and don't try to overload or to preach a sermon. Most of the time, the fewer words you use, the more will be remembered. Look for opportunities to gently encourage and comfort with the Word of God.

Help the Person Face Her Feelings

Don't tell a person how she should feel, but as feelings are expressed, listen and accept what is said. Many have particular difficulty with feelings of anger toward themselves, the person who left, and God as well. Reassure the person that these feelings are normal. It is okay to face the anger, the hurt, the pain. Remind her that God understands her feelings—that He experiences anger and grief, too—that He, too, is hurting with her. Help the person find appropriate ways to express her feelings, particularly anger.

Support groups have helped many face and express feelings. Find out what kinds of support groups are available in your area. Some churches sponsor "suddenly single" groups, as well as other supportive ministries. If there is no appropriate group in your area, pray about starting one yourself.

Include Her in Activities

In working with widowed and divorced people, one of the most common complaints is that they are treated differently after their loss. Jean, a forty-five-year-old woman who had been divorced for six months, explained it in this way:

> It wasn't until Doug left me that I realized how much of my social life revolved around married couples. Now, I was the extra person—the odd number. My friends didn't quite know how to treat me. Sometimes I felt as if they were afraid of my now "single" state—that somehow they had to watch their men when I was around—that now I couldn't be trusted. I was included in our traditional gatherings less and less. Nothing was ever really said, but there was a definite change. It really hurt me deeply. I didn't understand it until I talked to other women who had gone through the same thing. Unfortunately, I didn't meet those women until just recently. It was hard enough coping with the divorce. I also had to cope with the loss of my friends!

It is sometimes awkward for others to know how to handle a person who is suddenly not part of a couple! As much as possible, be sensitive to her feelings and include her as much as you can. Ask her to meet you at the movie or to accompany you to a concert, exhibit, or party. You don't have to include her in all your plans, but feeling included in a circle of friends is important to most of us.

Be especially sensitive around special occasions. Don't

avoid talking about them with her, but do be aware that the holiday or occasion may stir up painful feelings.

Encourage a Grieving Person to Put Off Major Decisions

The first few months following a loss is not the best time for making major decisions. If possible, encourage your friend to avoid major changes or making life-changing decisions until the initial shock has passed, and she has had time to grieve.

The Do's and Don'ts of Helping

Do:	Don't:
Find things to do to help.	Smother the person with your helpfulness, so that she feels as if she has no control.
Make calls, go to the grocery, entertain young children.	Say, "You shouldn't feel like that!"
Listen and accept her feelings.	Talk a lot.
Be with the person. Your presence means more than words.	Avoid the person because you don't know what to say.
Avoid judgments.	Criticize the person she has lost.
Assure her of God's love.	Preach to her or discuss theology.
Remember her, even after the initial trauma has passed.	Be available just until the funeral is over or the divorce is final.

Sometimes the situation is such that these major decisions must be made, however. If decisions must be made immediately, help her to get the counsel of those with expertise or knowledge in the area concerned. Most find that they receive too much contradictory advice from well-meaning friends and relatives. A grieving person doesn't always have the emotional energy to sort through the varying opinions. Being sensitive to this need may involve helping her to get sound counsel from one who is not involved.

In the case of an untimely death, it is not helpful and even may be harmful to tell a grieving person, particularly a child, that God wanted the one who died to come to heaven to live. To one in the midst of grieving her loss, this can seem like a slap in the face. One man told me of the death of his father when he was only twelve. He said:

> I was very close to my dad and loved him very much. There was an accident one day, and I was told that he had died and gone to heaven. I was devastated! I couldn't believe my dad was really gone. Sometime before the funeral, a kindly lady from the church came by the house. She said to me, "Larry, don't be sad. Your daddy is with God. God must have needed him in heaven more than you needed him here." Instead of that bringing me comfort, I was crushed. Didn't God know how much *I* needed my daddy? It took me a long time to trust God after that. I know that lady meant no harm, but I felt as if I had been robbed, not only of a daddy, but also of a loving heavenly Father!

Don't try to explain the whys to a grieving person. When she asks "Why did this happen?" don't attempt a lengthy theological explanation. Just say, "I don't know, but I am here." You are God's presence to that person. It's not your job to figure out all the answers. Your job is to love.

Ways to Help a Child

When you are faced with a grieving child, certain factors are very important, in addition to the other ways you can help.

Be Honest

No matter how young the child, talk to her about what is happening or going to happen. Be as honest as you can relating the facts. With young children, there is no need to go into the whys and wherefores, but instead prepare them for the change.

Tim was five years old when his parents divorced. Neither parent told him they were separating. One day, his father was gone and never came back.

> I remember asking my mother when Dad was coming home. I don't remember her giving me an answer, and I began to wonder what terrible thing had happened. Was he dead? Had he gotten mad at me and left? Didn't he love me anymore? Was my Mom going to leave me, too? I was confused, then later angry. Why couldn't someone have told me something?

Many parents, in an effort to protect the child, don't tell her they are divorcing, or that one parent has a terminal illness, or that the family is getting ready to move or make a major life change. Whether or not anything is said, however, children pick up on the nonverbal cues and tensions in the family. Tell a child as much as she can understand and is appropriate for her age. A child usually knows much more than the parent realizes. Don't try to protect her by lying to her or withholding pertinent information.

What About Me?

After you have told the child the basic facts, she will want to know: *"How will this affect me? Will we have to move? Are we poor now? Where will I go to school? Am I different from other kids now? What does this mean in my life?"*

Try to answer these questions as best you can. Assure her that no matter what changes occur, you love her and you will take care of her. If you don't know the answers to some of her questions, tell her you will give her the information as soon as you can.

"After you have told the child the basic facts, she will want to know 'How will this affect me?'"

If the child does not ask questions, do not assume she isn't wondering. Many times a child will not ask questions because she doesn't want to further upset the parent. Assume she wants to know, even if she doesn't ask, and talk to her.

Assure Her the Loss Is Not Her Fault

Because children and teenagers are self-absorbed, it is not unusual for a child to think that she caused or is the reason for the change. This is more likely when the change is sudden, and the child has not been prepared for the change.

Even if the facts seem clear to you as an adult, don't assume a child isn't attributing the death, divorce, or change to something she did or failed to do. Assure the child that she is not to blame.

Let Her Participate

Let the child participate in the change as much as is appropriate for her age. For example, if the change involves a move, let her study maps, visit the new neighborhood, and in some way, have some input into the process. If the change involves the death of a pet, let the child say good-bye to his pet in whatever way he chooses. Remember the importance of ceremonies!

In the case of the death of a close family member or friend, let the child, except in the case of a very young child, attend the funeral. You may think the child is too young to understand or will be frightened; but it is important for her to be able to participate, unless she doesn't want to do so. Most young children don't understand death very well and don't view funerals in the same manner as older children and adults.

By letting a young child attend the funeral, the parent has a point of reference for a child's later questions about death. For example, if a child asks, "Is Mommy coming home?" the parent can refer to the service and explain death in a manner the child can grasp.

In the case of an older child or teenager, ask her if she would like to help plan part of the service. Is there a song she would like to have sung? Let her pick out flowers to place on the casket or grave. Give her the opportunity to participate and to feel a part of the good-bye.

Let Your Feelings Show

Don't try to protect your child by hiding your own feelings. If she sees you expressing your feelings, she will be freer to express her own feelings.

Try to Keep the Same Routines

In any change, children seem to adjust more rapidly if routines remain the same as much as possible. If possible, the child should be given time to adjust before changing neighborhoods or schools. Try to follow as much of the child's routine as before. Routine gives a child a sense of security.

The Promises of God

Through the entire grief process, your friend can cling to
God's promises. When everyone else fails her, help her
know that she is never far from Him.

I Understand

[Jesus was] made like His brethren in every respect, in
order that He might become a merciful (sympathetic)
and faithful High Priest . . . For because He Himself [in
His humanity] has suffered . . . He is able [immediately]
to run to the cry of (assist, relieve) those who are . . .
[suffering]. (Hebrews 2:17–18)

He was despised and rejected and forsaken by men, a
Man of sorrows and pains, and acquainted with grief and
sickness; and like One from Whom men hide their faces
He was despised, and we did not appreciate His worth or
have any esteem for Him. (Isaiah 53:3)

I Am with You

Fear not [there is nothing to fear], for I am with you; do
not look around you in terror and be dismayed, for I am
your God. I will strengthen and harden you to difficulties, yes, I will help you; yes, I will hold you up and retain you with My [victorious] right hand of rightness and
justice. (Isaiah 41:10)

. . . for He [God] Himself has said, I will not in any way
fail you nor give you up nor leave you without support. [I
will] not, [I will] not, [I will] not in any degree leave you
helpless nor forsake nor let [you] down (relax My hold on
you)! [Assuredly not!] (Hebrews 13:5)

I Will Take Care of You

> And my God will liberally supply (fill to the full) your every need according to His riches in glory in Christ Jesus. (Philippians 4:19)

> For I know the thoughts and plans that I have for you, says the Lord, thoughts and plans for welfare and peace and not for evil, to give hope in your final outcome. (Jeremiah 29:11)

The greatest thing, ultimately, you can do for a person who is grieving is to point them toward the Source of all comfort, God the Father, Jesus the Son, and the Holy Spirit. The Words of God will work in her spirit, doing what no amount of human words can do (Hebrews 4:12).

LIFE APPLICATIONS

1. Has anyone who was close to you died? What were some of your reactions? What were some things that people did that were helpful to you? What was the least helpful thing someone said or did?

2. What are some of the "losses" you have experienced in your life? How did you "get through" these times? What was helpful? What wasn't?

3. Can you recall a time when you or someone you know experienced "unhealthy grief"? Why was it unhealthy? What did you do?

4. Have you ever known anyone who seemed to enjoy

their misfortune? How do you normally respond to people like that? Do you think you could help someone like this? Why or why not?

5. Have you ever felt pressured to give a person reasons why a "bad thing" happened? Does knowing why help? How can you go on, if you never know the reason?

6. Do you feel like your presence is enough when someone is grieving?

7. What are some ways you can help adults as well as children who are grieving?

8. Optional Exercise: With a partner, role play the do's and don'ts of helping found in the chapter. Take turns being the helper and being the one who is grieving.

9

BETRAYAL

And as they were eating, He said, Solemnly
I say to you, one of you will betray Me!
MATTHEW 26:21

All of us have been betrayed by another person. Whether betrayal is monumental or insignificant, degrees of shock and pain are the result. Betrayal causes us to lose faith in others, to despair, to build emotional walls of protection, or to distrust.

As you work with others, you will find that betrayal is a common problem. How can you help a friend who has been betrayed? How can you help a friend who has betrayed someone else? Can relationships be restored? Can trust be regained?

What Is Betrayal?

Wiping tears from his eyes, John informed me his wife had been unfaithful. Then there was an eerie silence as he stared into space. He appeared frozen in his chair. As I sat waiting, his thoughts seemed to travel far away, to wander and get lost somehow in his mind. When I spoke softly to him, he appeared not to hear. He finally turned to me and said, "I would never have believed Alice would have betrayed me like this! I've always trusted her! How could she have done this? And how could I have been so blind? I just can't believe this has happened!"

Betrayal comes in many forms, but the essence of betrayal is denial or abandonment in time of need, violation of a confidence, proof of false friendship, or deliverance into the hand of an enemy. John knew that his wife had abandoned him, violated her vows to him, and deceived him. He felt helpless in the grip of distrust, anger, and pain.

Since betrayal involves a loss, the pain of betrayal is similar to the grief that follows a death (see chapter 8: "Grief"). However, there is one distinct difference. Betrayal is the result of a *deliberate, voluntary* action. Betrayal is not accidental, although the actions of the betrayer may have been impulsive or due to some degree of ignorance. A person betrays someone else when another relationship or situation becomes more important to the betrayer than the first relationship.

Why Do People Betray?

Although betrayal is voluntary, varied and often confusing reasons are at its root.

Sitting in front of me, Alice looked as anguished as her husband, John, had looked hours earlier. "I don't know how it happened," she told me tearfully. "I never meant to hurt John. I've never been unfaithful to him before. I never thought I would! Before I knew what was happening, I was caught up in the situation, and I guess I just didn't think!"

Betrayal can be caused by a lack of moral character,

pressure from circumstances or people, or simply an attack from Satan. However, at the root of every betrayal is *self*. A person considers what *he* or *she* wants, even when it is at the expense of another person. When one person betrays another, he or she doesn't stop to evaluate how his or her actions will affect others. Self—and his or her own selfish desires—reigns supreme.

"Betrayal is the result of a deliberate, voluntary action. Betrayal is not accidental, although the actions of the betrayer may have been impulsive or due to some degree of ignorance."

When selfish ambition rules, betrayal occurs in a business relationship. When jealousy occurs, betrayal may happen in a friendship. If insecurity reigns, an unhealthy competitiveness can develop which will gradually turn one person against another. Lust for what we do not have will cause a person to steal, whether the object is material or another human being. Self grasps for what it wants at the expense of others.

Ways to Help the One Betrayed

If your friend is the one betrayed, you should consider these points in counseling her.

Be Available to Listen

Initially, your friend may not be able to speak fluently or may not want to talk at all. Many times the one who has been betrayed blames herself. In fact, she may not want you to know about the betrayal because of false pride and false guilt.

Whether or not she wants to talk, be available to listen. Don't be alarmed if she alternates between silence and rage. Remember, she is dealing with a loss, and she will experience a variety of grief reactions. Constantly affirm your understanding and loyalty. Pray for the wisdom to walk *with* her through her feelings and decisions.

Point Your Friend to Jesus

Although you may not have experienced the same situation your friend is facing, you can assure her that Jesus has felt the pain of betrayal. Matthew's account of Jesus' betrayal by Judas is vivid:

> As He was still speaking, Judas, one of the Twelve [apostles], came up, and with him a great crowd with swords and clubs, from the chief priests and elders of the people. Now the betrayer had given them a sign, saying, The One I shall kiss is the Man; seize Him. And he came up to Jesus at once and said, Hail (greetings, good health to You, long life to You), Master! And he embraced Him and kissed Him with [pretended] warmth and devotion. Jesus said to him, Friend, for what are you here? Then they came up and laid hands on Jesus and arrested Him. (Matthew 26:47–50)

After the arrest of Jesus, "all the disciples deserted Him and, fleeing, escaped" (Matthew 26:56). Jesus knew well the pain of betrayal from His closest and dearest friends.

Because the hurt from betrayal can be so devastating, your friend may feel as if God Himself has also betrayed her. Let her know that Jesus experienced that same feeling when He cried on the cross, "My God, My God, why have you abandoned Me [leaving Me helpless, forsaking Me, and failing Me in my need]?" (Matthew 27:46). Although God had not forsaken Jesus, Jesus did experience a time of separation from God as He took our sins upon Himself. He knew what it was like to feel as if He were forsaken.

Remind your friend that in the anguish of betrayal, she can cry out to Jesus. By His Holy Spirit, He will come and comfort her. If Jesus did not offer His comfort, we could barely survive the blow of betrayal, and we would be without hope for the future. The One who experienced betrayal and overcame the emotions it produced can be the perfect physician to our emotions. He applies the peace that passes understanding as a balm when we come to Him (John 14:27).

Be Reliable

This is a time when the question, "How could I have been so blind?" will replay itself in your friend's mind, causing her to suspect even those who have not betrayed her. As I talked with John, he began to question not only Alice's loyalty, but also the trustworthiness of *all* his friends. "If I didn't see what Alice was doing, what else have I overlooked? Whom can I trust? Maybe everyone has known about it! I feel like such a fool!"

Keep your word without fail, reassuring her that you will keep her confidences. Be reliable in small ways, such as promptness and calling exactly when you promise, because anxiety will flare easily during her recovery.

Caution Her Against Prolonged Anger

As soon as your friend appears to be willing, talk with her about the harm of prolonged anger. Point out the spiritual, emotional, and physical toll anger exacts (see chapters 6: "Anger," and 11: "Bitterness"). Suggest that she write out her feelings until she has nothing left to express. Offer to be with her when she expresses those feelings one last time to God, asking Him to cleanse her mind and body of the effects of anger and to refresh her total being.

Discourage Ruminations

Although your friend will need time to talk through her betrayal and her feelings, she will reach a point when this becomes destructive and self-indulgent. If your friend begins to repeat her past story, focusing on the wrongs done to her and seems resistant to looking at healing and restoration, gently ask her why she thinks that repeating it will help her. If she cannot give you a valid reason, suggest that you direct your attention toward prayer for healing, as well as to alternatives that will make her present life productive.

Guide Her in the Process of Forgiveness

Although your friend may resist, you must talk with her about forgiving the person who betrayed her (see chapter 11: "Bitterness"). Remind her that forgiving her betrayer simply involves letting go of the anger and resentment. It does not mean that she was not wronged.

Look at Alternatives

As your friend's anger diminishes, ask her what she believes God wants her to do. Set a specific time to pray together about her alternatives, reminding her that Jesus knows how she feels and that He will come to her aid.

For her own well-being, she must be willing to go through the process of healing and deliverance from her problem *in God's way*. Whether or not forgiveness seems fair, she must forgive. She will need to turn her mind toward Jesus in praise for His presence, willingness, and ability to help her and for His desire to give her a good and abundant life. Continually point your friend to Jesus, who overcame His own betrayal, was raised to glorify His Father, and constantly intercedes for us. Remind her that the same power that raised Jesus from the dead lives within her (Ephesians 1:19–20). If she will resist the desire for revenge and the temptation to bitterness, she will be healed and delivered from her pain.

Ways to Help the Betrayer

When the person you counsel has betrayed a friend, your role is also clearly defined. She too feels the weight of the betrayal.

Offer Love, Not Judgment

The apostle John tells of a confrontation between Jesus and the scribes and Pharisees who had caught a woman in the act of adultery. Jewish law required that the woman be stoned, so trying to trick Jesus, these religious leaders asked Him what they should do. Jesus said to them, "Let him who is without sin among you be the first to throw a stone at her" (John 8:7). Jesus did not condone the sin the woman had committed, but He did not judge her. Instead, He offered her an alternative, saying, "Go on your way and from now on sin no more" (John 8:11).

As you work with a friend who has betrayed someone else, it will be tempting to judge her, especially if you do not understand the reasons for her actions.

There is, however, a time to "judge," in the sense that you must ultimately decide whether to continue your involvement with your friend. The woman caught in adultery had a choice—she could obey Jesus and "sin no more," or she could return to her former lifestyle.

Scripture is specific about how to respond to someone who does not want to turn away from a sin. A person within the Corinthian church continued to engage in a sexual sin after having been warned and confronted with his sin. Paul instructed the church to avoid him and not allow him to fellowship in the church as long as he refused to repent (1 Corinthians 5). The purpose was not to be cruel, but rather to help him see the emptiness of his sin so that he would want to change.

Be very careful about making rash judgments about your friend's motives and heart. Offer the compassion, love, and forgiveness of Jesus. But realize there is a point at which you may have to dissociate yourself from your friend if she is unwilling to change a sinful behavior.

Guide Her in the Process of Forgiveness

If your friend expresses genuine sorrow for the hurt she has caused, guide her in asking God's forgiveness, as well as the forgiveness from the one whom she has betrayed. David wrote Psalm 51 after he had been confronted about his sins of adultery and murder. It is an excellent example of a prayer for forgiveness and cleansing.

If your friend feels too guilty to ask for God's help, remind her that Jesus knew that she would betray, just as He knew and told Peter that he would betray Him three times before the crucifixion (Matthew 26:34). Assure her that forgiveness is available for her, just as it was for Peter.

Help Your Friend to Make a Plan

Is restitution necessary? Does she need to ask others for forgiveness? Can steps be taken toward healing? How can she ensure she won't sin again in this way? How can she begin to rebuild trust?

I could tell that Alice was truly sorry for the pain she had caused John. She confessed her sin to God and received forgiveness. As she felt the need to talk to him, she cried, "I don't know what I can say! How can he ever forgive me for what I have done?" As we talked, we were able to identify some of the problems in the marriage that had preceded Alice's betrayal. She began to realize her mistakes and to understand how to prevent them from occurring in the future. "I see some things I could have done differently. I don't ever want to make those same mistakes again. Do you think if I told John what I have realized and what I will do in the future, that he could begin to forgive me and trust me again?" As Alice made specific plans for future responses and identified her own weaknesses and strengths, she began to feel new hope.

> ## "A built-in system of accountability will help restore trust and provide security for your friend."

Help your friend to take responsibility for her behavior and to identify any steps she can initiate to bring healing to the person she has betrayed. Identify specific steps she can take to guard against another betrayal. Encourage her to ask God to place His light in the recesses of her mind so that she can be cleansed in those areas of weakness.

Hold Her Accountable

A betrayer will not only find it difficult to be trusted by the person whom she injured, but she will also have trouble trusting herself. A built-in system of accountability will help restore trust and provide security for your friend. Without accountability, chances are slim that trust will ever be regained. Accountability will reduce opportunities for suspicion. Although love may be freely given, trust must be earned.

Frank said, "My business partner expected me to forget what he had done just because he said he was sorry! I think I'd be a fool to do that! He almost ruined our company by altering our books! Surely I can't be expected to take another chance like that!"

Frank decided not to dissolve the partnership, but instead he asked him to submit weekly financial reports. Through seeing months of honest accounting, Frank was able to choose to trust his partner again. If his partner had not proven himself trustworthy, Frank would have had no reason to trust.

If, however, your friend resists accountability, then trust with the injured party cannot be easily restored. If she refuses to be accountable, ask, "Is there some reason why you are unwilling to earn the trust you have lost?" Many times the problem is pride from which stubbornness springs. Becoming accountable to another person requires genuine humility, as well as the recognition that regaining trust may be a long process. Not everyone who betrays is willing to become humble and accept the process required.

After your friend is willing to become accountable, and

the one whom she betrayed has forgiven her, work on a plan of accountability with both of them. Identify the areas of greatest fear, and help them to agree how to gradually overcome specific fears.

Ask your friend to call you if she is ever tempted to commit the same sin again. Be willing to listen, encourage, admonish, and strengthen with prayer and God's Word.

Alice decided that when she was on trips or in other situations in which temptations would be great, she would call a friend of hers to pray for her. She told me, "Last week I had to go out of town for two nights. Before I left, I called Sally and asked her to pray for me while I was gone. I told her I wanted to be held accountable for what I did on the trip and wanted to call her when I returned. Knowing I had promised to be open with her helped me to feel more confident that I could do the right thing. Facing tempting possibilities ahead of time is helping to warn me, and knowing my friends are praying for me has given me strength."

When your friend calls you during a time of temptation, express confidence in her, reminding her of other times when she has resisted temptation. Pray for her to be filled with the Holy Spirit. Ask God to protect her from Satan's attacks on her life.

Encourage Her to Seek Support from Others

Most temptations and problems are too overpowering for us to struggle with alone. Wise Solomon said, "Two are better than one, because they have a good [more satisfying] reward for their labor; For if they fall, the one will lift up his fellow. But woe to him who is alone when he falls and has not another to lift him up!" (Ecclesiastes 4:9–10). Encourage your friend to surround herself with other Christians who will support her with prayer and encouragement. Remind her, too, that as she supports others, she will be supported.

The Process of Restoration

Betrayal not only occurs in marriages, but also in friendships, business relationships, ministries, as well as between parents and children. Regardless of what type of relationship has been violated by betrayal, the process of restoration will seem impossible at first for both the betrayed and the betrayer. Before restoration can begin, each must decide whether she wants the relationship restored. It may take time for each of the parties to gain the strength necessary to reinvest in the relationship.

Only God knows the future and can guide wounded partners forward. Restoration is possible in most cases, but success depends on the desire of *both* parties. Allow time for God to give them His desire for the relationship.

If both do possess the desire to restore the relationship, then help them through the steps of the restoration process.

Repentance

The first step of restoration is repentance on the part of the betrayer (see chapter 12: "Guilt"). There must be true sorrow for the hurt she has caused toward the betrayed party and toward God. Repentance is more than being sorry; *repentance means to be sorry enough to change the behavior.*

Forgiveness

Forgiveness is the second step in the restoration process. The betrayer must ask God's forgiveness, as well as forgiveness of the one she betrayed.

Forgiveness involves not only the betrayer, but also the betrayed. If your friend was betrayed, she must become willing to forgive. It is tempting to want revenge or to engage in self-protective measures, such as withdrawal, bitterness, or vengeful acts. At this point, much prayer will be required, because both parties will be at a crossroads. Emotions will be so tattered and worn that any action will have great impact. A decision should be made carefully, according to God's Word, after much prayer for healing, self-control, and wisdom. At such a critical point, an impulsive, misguided action can be the "last straw" that kills a second chance for reconciliation.

Time

Each partner must allow time for healing and trust to develop. Healing and trust are not regained in a day.

Months after I first talked with him, John confided, "When I finally forgave Alice for the affair, I somehow thought I should be able to trust her immediately just because she was so sorry. But, when she would be late coming home from work, I would worry. When I became anxious, I would meet her at the door with 'Where have you been? I was worried!' She got really irritated with me and answered, 'I thought you said you would trust me!' When this scenario continued over the weeks, I became chronically suspicious, and she became chronically angry! I guess this all takes time!"

Understanding

Understanding how the betrayal began can be an aid in the restoration process. "How could this have happened?" and "How could you have done this to me?" are questions that sometimes need to be answered. An understanding of what happened can give the security to both parties that there may be some way to prevent another betrayal. Knowledge increases chances of prevention.

With fear in his voice, Joe said, "My wife deceived me about our credit cards. I thought our monthly bills were paid, and now I've found that we owe thousands of dollars! How could she have spent money we didn't have? I believe she means it when she promises never to do it again, but how can I trust her? If she did it once, why won't she do it again? I never thought she'd do it the first time! She's really ashamed of what she did, but how do I know she won't fool herself again? What if I fool myself, too? I don't trust either of us!"

Joe had not only lost faith in his wife's ability to make sound judgments, but he had lost faith in his own ability to discern the truth. He was afraid to trust her with credit cards, and he was afraid to trust his decision to give her access to credit cards in the future.

Joe asked his wife why she began to use credit cards so carelessly. As he listened, he realized that she had felt very insecure when she entertained his business associates in their home, so she had bought china and household accessories to enhance the appearance of their home. He heard the fear and guilt in her voice as she continued to explain her buying, knowing that she was placing their family in debt, realizing that exposure was soon to come. Joe realized for the first time how much pressure he had placed on his wife.

Although she had betrayed him through her deceit and dishonesty, Joe had begun to understand her weakness. By humbling themselves before God, as well as each other, they were able to forgive and find ways to work together to reduce the strain she felt, thus relieving the temptation to overspend.

With a sincere desire for resolution on the part of both parties, repentance, forgiveness, time, and understanding, restoration is possible. As you work with friends, help them to draw on the power of the Father for strength, help, and endurance. He will enable them to repent, forgive, understand, and He will sustain them through the process time.

The Blessing from Betrayal

Until we are face to face with the betrayal of someone we have completely trusted, we cannot truly realize the need to lean totally on Jesus. It is easier for us to rely on a human being whom we can see, hear, feel, and touch—until that person fails us. Then we have a need to draw more closely to Jesus, who is the only Person upon whom we can rely totally. Suddenly, we become convinced of the frailty of the commitment of human beings one to another, and we *know* that there is only One who will never disappoint us.

God's Word states: "Lean on, trust in, and be confident in the Lord with all your heart and mind and do not rely on your own insight or understanding. In all your ways know, recognize, and acknowledge Him, and He will direct and make straight and plain your paths" (Proverbs 3:5–6).

God does not intend for us to rely on one another or on ourselves more than we rely on Him. Leaning on Him for our help and strength will bring us through any circumstance of life, and we can say with Habakkuk:

> The Lord God is my Strength, my personal bravery, and my invincible army; He makes my feet like hinds' feet and will make me to walk [not to stand still in terror, but to walk] and make [spiritual] progress upon my high places [of trouble, suffering, or responsibility]! (Habakkuk 3:19)

LIFE APPLICATIONS _____

1. Have you ever been betrayed by anyone close to you? How did you feel when you first found out?

2. What was the first thing you wanted to do when you learned you had been betrayed? Did you do it? What happened?

3. Were you tempted to blame yourself for the betrayal? Why?

4. Have you found it tempting to "replay" hurtful events in your own life? Has this helped?

5. Why does the suggestion of forgiveness provoke so much initial resistance?

6. How can you refrain from judging while making it clear that you do not condone a sin?

7. How does accountability help us in everyday life? How can it be useful to rebuild trust?

8. Can you trust someone again who doesn't appear to really regret what they have done?

9. Have you ever been defeated by an unrecognized weakness? Give an example.

10. Memorize Habakkuk 3:19.

10

ABUSE

. . . a broken spirit dries up the bones.

PROVERBS 17:22

I've been depressed for as long as I can remember. I have a good life, so there's no *reason* for me to be depressed. What is wrong with me?"

"I'm so ashamed. I'm a terrible wife. Otherwise, my husband wouldn't hit me and call me names. How can I be a better wife?"

"My dad physically abused me when I was growing up, and I swore I would never do that to my own children! But last night, it happened. I slapped my two-year-old! I'm so afraid! What if I turn out to be just like my dad?"

Child abuse statistics are alarming. Not only are the incidences of child abuse increasing, but so are reports of spouse abuse and other types of family violence. The more you counsel others, the more you will uncover emotional, physical, or sexual abuse, by parents, relatives, friends, spouses, or strangers.

What is abuse? How can you help someone who has been abused? What should you do if you think your friend may be abusing her own children? How can you help a victim of spouse abuse?

What Is Abuse?

Before you can help someone with a problem, the problem must be recognized. Many who have suffered from abusive situations, especially emotional abuse and neglect, are *unaware that they have been abused*. They are under the impression that all families are like their own. Not having had close contact with healthy families, they are astounded to realize they were abused or that they are abusing their own children! Many spouses do not know that they have a right to feel safe in their own homes. It is important for you to know what constitutes abuse so you can help your friend recognize and acknowledge abuse in her life.

Physical Abuse

Physical abuse is any physical mistreatment of a child that is not accidental or any type of corporal punishment that causes bruises or other injuries.

Katie told of a childhood filled with abuse from her mother. She said, "When Mother was really mad, she would make me stand in the bathtub, and she would whip me with an electrical cord. I would have welts on my skin, and sometimes bruises. Other times, she would make me stand on one foot in the corner, and when I couldn't keep my balance, she would hit me. Until I was older, I thought all children were punished this way."

Physical abuse also includes hitting a child with anything, such as cords, ropes, belts, and even hands with enough force or repetition that results in marks, bruises, breaking of the skin, broken bones, or fractures. Slapping or hitting a child with the hand or fist, throwing a child against a wall or object, burning a child with cigarettes, or biting a child are all physically abusive behaviors.

Emotional Abuse

Emotional abuse can be equally as harmful as physical abuse, although the marks are not as visible. Emotional abuse can consist of a single incident or it can be a pattern of behavior. Examples of emotional abuse include harsh threatening, ridiculing, belittling, frightening, continual teasing or humiliating, or making a child a scapegoat for family problems.

Another type of emotional abuse, sometimes not so easily recognized, is emotional neglect—what *wasn't* done.

"My dad was a minister, and it never occurred to me that he was emotionally abusive," the petite redhead said with surprise. "I don't remember his ever hugging me or telling me he loved me, but Mother wasn't affectionate either, so I didn't think anything about it. Neither of them were mean—they just weren't there for me emotionally. I never considered that was abuse. I just thought there was something wrong with me. After all, they seemed to be there for everyone else!"

"Many who have suffered from abusive situations, especially emotional abuse and neglect, are unaware that they have been abused. They are under the impression that all families are like their own."

Emotional abuse includes not only saying hurtful things to a child, such as "I wish you'd never been born," or "You're no good," but also includes covert rejections such as not providing emotional security, nurturing, or love, as well as controlling a child through guilt or withdrawal of parental approval.

Sexual Abuse

Sexual abuse is sexual contact between a child and adult or child and older child. It includes actual *physical contact* with the child, ranging from touching or fondling a child's genitals or breasts or having the child touch the offender, to oral sex and attempted or actual penetration of the vagina or rectum. Sexual abuse also includes *non-physical contact*, such as exposure of a child's or offender's genitals, sexually explicit speech in front of a child, or exploitation through pornography or prostitution.

"I was about five when my stepdad started abusing me," began the attractive, poised woman sitting across from me. "I didn't know what he was doing was wrong—I thought all daddies played 'secret games' with their little girls. He started out by giving me 'baths,' then making me give him baths, too. I didn't like touching him or his touching me, but I didn't know what to do. I felt bad about what we were doing, but he never tried to do anything else to me, so I just thought there was something wrong with me. By the time I realized other dads weren't like mine, I was too ashamed to tell anybody what had been happening."

It is common for victims of sexual abuse to minimize the damage done to them if penetration did not actually occur. But remember, sexual abuse is very harmful and can leave deep scars, no matter how "mild" or "severe" the abuse seems.

The Effects of Abuse

The effects of abuse are far-reaching. You will see many who suffer from depression, have difficulty trusting others, or are fearful. Your friend may not tell you she was abused, partly because she may not be aware that her problems stem from past abuse.

If you think your friend might have been abused, discuss some of the following questions from *My Father's Child* (pp. 7–8). All deal with common effects of past abuse:

1. Do you have trouble trusting people?

2. Do you feel guilty and ashamed but don't know why?

3. Have you engaged in self-destructive behaviors such as alcohol or drug abuse, suicidal gestures, or destructive relationships?

4. Are you frequently depressed?

5. Do you hate certain members of your family?

6. Do you lose your temper easily and become verbally or physically hurtful?

7. Do other people think you look angry (or sad) when you're really not feeling that way?

8. Do you feel you were cheated out of or denied a childhood?

9. Do you have few close friends?

10. Do you have a hard time relaxing or having fun?

11. Do you have many fears?

12. Do you think other people wouldn't like you if they knew you?

13. Do you often feel that you don't measure up?

14. Have you had problems in your marriage or in relationships with the opposite sex?

15. Are you overweight or do you feel that you are unattractive?

16. Do you often find yourself hating the way you act toward others?

17. Do you often feel rejected by others?

18. Are you overly critical of yourself and others?

19. Is your relationship with your family strained?

20. Do you often regret things you have said or done?

21. Are you often disappointed in yourself?

22. Do you remember bruises or marks on your body following punishment?

23. Do you frequently act on impulse?

24. Do you have difficulty remembering your childhood?

25. Do you distrust or discount God's love for you?

If your friend answers "yes" to many of these questions, she may be suffering from the effects of child abuse.

The Issue of Trust

Before you can begin to help a person who has been abused or who is abusing her children, a level of trust must be established. Those who have been hurt at the hands of others have trouble trusting others. Don't be upset if your friend is fearful of your rejection or has difficulty believing you or trusting you. If she has been rejected, not believed, and abused by those she trusted as a child, she will have little reason to think that you are different from them.

It is very important to be gentle and patient with victims of abuse. You will need to assure your friend that she will be heard, understood, and helped. Because most abuse victims believe the abuse was their fault, your friend may be hesitant to tell you what happened, for fear that you will also blame and reject her. You will need to consistently re-affirm your loyalty and desire to help.

When she begins to tell you her story, you may find that your friend has a difficult time talking about her feelings or that she talks about what has happened to her in a voice devoid of emotion—as if the abuse happened to someone else. This is normal. Many victims have learned to separate themselves from the abuse in order to survive. You need to let her know you are "hearing" her feelings and that what she is feeling is all right. You may want to make comments, such as "I'm so sorry that happened to you," or "That must have really hurt." Most abuse victims don't think their feelings are valid. As you assure your friend that you believe her and that you won't reject her, the trust between you will grow.

Ways to Help Someone Who Has Been Abused

When your friend begins to face her own abuse as a child, she will need your guidance in handling her emotions. Healing will come only after painful memories are confronted.

Why Did God Let Me Be Abused?

The only basis for long-term healing from the effects of abuse is through a relationship with God, so one of the first questions you need to address is, "If God loved me, why did He let me be abused?" Your friend will be unable to trust God for her healing as long as she believes that God wanted her to be abused.

"Most abuse victims don't think their feelings are valid."

One woman commented, "I thought God allowed me to be abused so I would know how to help other people whose parents had abused them." Another added, "I thought God just didn't care. I prayed and prayed for Him to make my dad quit hitting me and sexually molesting me, but it went on until I left home. By that time, I decided there wasn't a God—or if there was, I definitely didn't want to know Him!"

Be certain that your friend realizes that abuse of any kind is not God's will. God hates abuse! Our Father is a God of love who instructs us to love one another, not to bring harm.

Help your friend understand that her *abuser, not God, is responsible* for the abuse. When God created us, He gave us the freedom of choice. God placed Adam in the Garden of Eden and said, "You may freely eat of every tree of the garden; But of the tree of the knowledge of good and evil and blessing and calamity you shall not eat, for in the day that you eat of it you shall surely die" (Genesis 2:16–17).

God limited the use of His control over us when He gave man the right to choose. The hurt that we cause one another in this world is not due to God's choice; it is due to the misuse of our right to choose. When we choose wrongly, we sin. Abuse is sin, and God hates abuse!

Help your friend to realize that abuse is always the choice and will of the abuser—it is *never* the choice and will of God!

Identifying the Lies

Those who were abused believe many lies about themselves, others, and life. You will need to listen carefully, help your friend to identify her false beliefs, and guide her to substitute what is true. Some of the most common lies believed by those who were abused are:

1. The abuse was my fault.

2. Since the abuse was my fault, I deserve to be punished.

3. I don't measure up. I am a failure.

4. I must not fail.

5. Trusting people is dangerous. I mustn't get close to people.

6. Feelings are bad. I mustn't show my feelings.

7. People are no good. I am no good. I hate them. I hate me.

8. Everything wrong in my life is their fault.

In addition to these lies, those who have been sexually abused may also believe:

1. If I make myself sexually unappealing, I can avoid further abuse. Being unattractive will protect me.

2. Sexual contact is the only way to get my needs met.

3. Nobody will ever care as much for me as he does. I'll always care about him. I owe him that.

4. I don't want the sexual relationship with him, but if I can't have him, I don't want anyone else to have him either.

5. My body is disgusting. I hate my body!

One woman who came to counseling for problems in her marriage related, "When I was thirteen, I was molested by my older brother and one of his friends. I remember feeling humiliated and embarrassed as they made me take off my clothes. When they began touching me, I felt so ashamed because, in spite of my anger, what they were doing felt good! I felt a dark sense of shame come over me. I decided then to make myself so unattractive that nobody would want to do that to me again. I gained fifty pounds in three months. I have hated my body ever since! My body betrayed me!"

Learning to believe the truth is a process which can be difficult if many of the lies have been reinforced since childhood. Don't get discouraged if your friend has difficulty believing the truth. Continue to remind her of God's truth, and be patient if it takes time for the "head knowledge" to be transformed into "heart knowledge." Remind her and yourself of the words of Jesus, "And you will know the Truth, and the Truth will set you free" (John 8:32).

As you counsel with your friend, I recommend asking her to read the first four chapters in the book *My Father's Child* (Brentwood, TN: Wolgemuth and Hyatt, 1988).

These chapters specifically address these common lies and point the reader to an understanding of God's truth.

The Necessity of Forgiveness

Forgiveness is a very important step in the healing process, but it is also one that many resist. For those who have been hurt deeply, it is difficult to justify reasons to forgive those who have assaulted them. Many know that Jesus commanded us to forgive, but they do not realize that the act of forgiveness will benefit *them*, too! Unforgiveness chains a victim to the past. Without a willingness to forgive those who have harmed her, your friend will not be able to receive God's healing. Forgiveness frees a person to receive from God!

Forgiveness is not forgetting; it is not saying the abuse was okay; it is not acting as if the abuse never occurred; it is not an act that will change the abuser. Forgiveness is letting go of the resentment and bitterness toward the abuser; it is a decision to forgive (In the name of Jesus, I will forgive _____ for _____); it is a joint effort with the Holy Spirit's power in her heart. Her part is to will to forgive; God's part is to complete the spiritual and emotional transaction of forgiveness.

You may find this verse encouraging as you help your friend forgive her abuser:

> [Not in your own strength] for it is God Who is all the while effectually at work in you [energizing and creating in you the power and desire], both to will and to work for His good pleasure and satisfaction and delight. (Philippians 2:13)

Don't be surprised if your friend becomes frustrated with you when you are firm about the necessity of forgiveness. Abused persons often perceive others as controlling and forceful and may even draw back from you and respond in fear.

Pray for patience. It is very difficult for someone to let go of an attitude they have had for a long time. Don't attempt to coerce her into forgiving, but continue to love and encourage her by reminding her of the benefits she will experience when she forgives her abuser. The process of forgiveness may be ongoing, so you may often refer to the need to forgive each time you see bitterness or resentment. (For further information on forgiveness, see chapter 11: "Bitterness.")

> **"Forgiveness is letting go of the resentment and bitterness toward the abuser; it is a decision to forgive."**

Ways to Help Someone Who Is Abusing Her Children

Many are reluctant to become involved with someone who is abusing her children. Until you have been involved with abusive parents, you may feel frightened.

Years ago, when I first began investigating cases of suspected child abuse, I would feel very frightened as I drove to the home of a suspected abuser. I just knew I was getting ready to encounter some type of violent monster! I wanted to go help the children, but I was also afraid she would abuse me!

One day I received a report about a mother of three small children. The caller said that all three children had cuts on their bodies from having been beaten with a tree limb. She described the cuts as "deep, caked with dried blood."

As I met this mother and told her why I had come, she began to cry, sinking down onto the steps of her front porch. I sat down beside her and she said, "I know I've done wrong! I hate to whip them this hard, but it's the only way I know to keep them in line!" She leaned forward, intently looking into my face, and continued, "I'm just doing what I learned from my grandfather! I don't know what else to do! Let me show you something!" Suddenly, she turned around and pulled her T-shirt up around her shoulders, exposing her entire back, which was filled with long, very wide scars. "This is what he did to me," she said. "I know how much it hurts to be beaten like this! I hate doing it, but these kids drive me crazy sometimes, and I just have to get them in line! What else can I do? I want to stop, but *I don't know anything else to do!*"

Look for the Reasons

No parent wants to abuse her child. Tremendous grief and guilt fill the heart of an abusing parent. Abuse is a cycle, extending from generation to generation. This cycle can be broken, but many parents simply do not know how to train their children in a constructive manner. Lack of knowledge, inadequate releases for anger, lack of problem-solving skills, ineffective discipline, and not feeling loved are all reasons parents abuse their children. Knowing that there *are* specific reasons behind abusive behavior will help you to offer hope to your friend. She isn't abusing her children because she is mean or hateful. She is abusing her children because she is still suffering from the effects of her own abuse.

Look for the reasons behind a parent's abusive behavior to help her find ways to address these causes.

Offer Compassion, Not Judgment

Remember that the abusing parent feels like an abused child inside an adult body. This will help you to offer compassion, rather than judgment.

Identify with her feelings in a loving way. For example, you might say, "It seems as if the children are getting you down. Do you need a break? What could we work out?"

Offer help without condescension. "It's hard to know what to do with your child when she acts like that, isn't it? When my boys were small, I found something that helped. Would you like to hear about it?"

Addressing your concerns in these ways will enable your friend to see that you care about her, as well as her children, and it will be easier for her to talk honestly.

Provide Protection for the Children

The safety of any child is your top priority. If you suspect that a child is being abused and your friend will not be open with you, be honest with her. Tell her what you think and why. Her initial reaction may be fear and anger, but she will be relieved later that the problem has been faced.

You need to report the abuse to the proper authorities in order to assure protection for the children and help for the parent. Your area may have a local agency that deals with child abuse. If you are not sure, call the Child Abuse and Neglect Hotline at 1-800-482-5964 (24 hours a day). They will tell you where to call.

Ways to Help Someone Who Is Being Abused by a Spouse

As the woman across from me poured out her fears and frustrations, her words belied her chic, expensively groomed appearance. Her skillfully applied make-up camouflaged the bruises and swelling under her right eye. To look at her, "battered wife" would have been the last thing I would have suspected.

She told her story with tears in her voice, all the while watching me anxiously for signs of disbelief or blame. For the past ten years, she had been periodically beaten by her husband, a successful physician in town. She had suffered a broken nose, broken fingers, and once a broken leg, as well as numerous bruises and abrasions from being pushed or hit in the face.

"I've never told anyone before," she whispered. "I've been so ashamed. I've tried and tried to be a good wife to my husband, but, no matter what I do, I can't seem to please him. I know if I were different, he would treat me better. He's a good man and a good father. He's always hugging the children, and he's never even raised his voice to them."

"I've thought about leaving," she continued, weeping openly now, "but who would I be without him? He's told me no one would want a wife like me, and he's probably right. My dad used to hit my sister and me at times, but that was only when we deserved it. I'm so tired of trying so hard and failing. I've come so close to just ending it all lately. Can you help me?"

Unfortunately, this woman's story is repeated in many homes across our country. Spouse abuse is a common, though carefully hidden activity. Many women who were abused by parents marry men who are also abusive, continuing the familiar pattern of mistreatment.

Usually the violent spouse threatens his partner in ways that make her afraid to ask for help or to leave. Although Judy was a registered nurse, she had been so emotionally beaten down by her husband that she was no longer confident in her professional nursing skills. She was afraid to ask for help, because she was sure no one would believe her, and because she thought she deserved the abuse.

Suspect spouse abuse if a woman:

- has visible cuts, bruises, black eyes, scratches, or other injuries that aren't consistent with her explanation ("I stumbled and fell");

- wears clothing that is out of season, such as wearing long sleeves in very hot weather;

- wears heavy make-up in an attempt to hide facial marks or bruises;

- seems hesitant to invite others to her house;

- appears fearful, on edge, withdrawn, or has frequent mood swings;

- has unexplained absences at functions, consistently misses appointments, or changes plans at the last minute;

- appears fearful of not pleasing her husband;

- is guarded and overprotective of her husband—excuses or justifies his behavior to others.

Offer Emotional Support

Most battered spouses are so frightened and beaten down—physically and emotionally—that they don't trust themselves to make good decisions anymore. Let her know that you believe her, that her spouse's actions are intolerable, and that you will help her. Assure her that she is not to blame for his actions and that she doesn't "deserve" mistreatment, even if she were the most horrible wife in the world! Let her know that you do not think she's crazy for "loving" her husband—but that she can love her husband and protect herself at the same time. Protecting herself from harm does not negate her love for him.

Offer Practical Support and Make a Plan

Tell your friend that specific help is available, and help her make a plan. Where can she go if her husband becomes violent? What warning signs precede his violence? What preparations can she make ahead of time?

Although reluctant to do so, she should consider medical treatment, and take pictures of her injuries, in order to document the abuse, should it recur.

What kind of job training would be helpful? What skills does she already possess? What are her financial needs?

Discussing these issues and making a plan that covers practical needs can provide her with a feeling of security, as well as help her define the problem and possible solutions.

If your friend will not seek safety for herself, it is important to assure her of your continued love and availability. (If her children are in direct danger, however, you will need to aggressively address their physical protection as outlined in the previous section of this chapter.) Let your friend know that whatever she chooses to do, you will be with her and you will love her. An excellent resource book to share with her is *Love Must Be Tough: New Hope for Families in Crisis* by Dr. James Dobson (Waco, TX: Word Books, 1983). In this book, he addresses what to do in abusive marital situations.

Find out what programs are available in your community for the abusive spouse. Most programs recommend that the abuser move out of the family home until he gets help. Let your friend know there is help available—for both her and her husband.

The Value of Support Groups

In my work with men and women who were abused, I have found support groups to be among the most effective instruments of God's healing. Support groups can offer encouragement, specific counseling related directly to abuse, and opportunities for ministry. I would encourage you to pray about forming an informal group. Included in the paperback edition of *My Father's Child* is a Guidebook with twelve structured sessions for those who have been abused. Pray about beginning a support group, using this as a resource.

And Most Important of All, Point to God

It is essential that your friend know that God cares and that He will never leave her. I have found these verses to have great impact on those who were (or are being) abused:

> Can a woman forget her nursing child, that she should not have compassion on the son of her womb? Yes, they may forget, yet I will not forget you. Behold, I have indelibly imprinted (tattooed a picture of) you on the palm of each of my hands. (Isaiah 49:15–16)

> Fear not [there is nothing to fear], for I am with you; do not look around you in terror and be dismayed, for I am your God. I will strengthen and harden you to difficul-

ties, yes, I will help you; yes, I will hold you up and retain you with My [victorious] right hand of rightness and justice. (Isaiah 41:10)

It is God's will to break the pattern of abuse, to heal the brokenhearted, to proclaim liberty to the captives of Satan's lies, and to free those who have been bound by the effects of past abuse (Isaiah 61:1). Working with those who have suffered abuse is one of the most rewarding ministries you will experience.

LIFE APPLICATIONS

1. Have you ever experienced an incident of physical, emotional, or sexual abuse? What were the results? How did you feel?

2. Why do you think God allows children to be abused? How would you explain this to a friend who had been abused?

3. How do you feel about parents who abuse their children? Do you feel you could feel compassionate toward parents who are abusing their children? Why or why not?

4. How do you feel about mates who beat their spouses? Have you ever wanted to hit your spouse or your children? What stopped you? What did you do instead?

5. Share an experience in which you had to forgive someone who had done a great wrong to you. How

did you do it? How did you feel after you had forgiven? Why do you think God commands us to forgive?

6. If you were abused, do you feel that you have experienced enough healing to help others who were abused? Are you still angry about your own childhood?

7. Are you able to back away from an intense situation, or do you tend to get "hooked" on a crisis? What are some things you can do to avoid burnout?

8. Where are the resources available in your community for those who are being abused?

11

BITTERNESS

> My wound is incurable, though I am without
> transgression. . . . It profits a man nothing
> that he should delight himself with
> God and consent to Him.
>
> JOB 34:6, 9

*L*ife has never treated me fairly! I've never been happy!
No matter how hard I work, I can never get ahead.
Someone always gets what I want. Why has God treated
me this way?"

Most of us know people who are bitter. They are easily
recognized. Their speech is whiny and filled with complaints. They have a rigid, bent countenance. They rarely,
if ever, smile from the eyes. They blame others and God for
their circumstances, their frown, a permanent fixture.

Bitterness is a serious problem, not only psychologically
but also physically and spiritually. A bitter person knows
no joy; she is usually tired and depleted. She may have
many aches and pains; a bitter person is cut off from a full
relationship with God and from receiving the full measure
of His blessings. How do you help a person who is bitter
toward another person? How can you help a person who is

bitter toward God? Can a person who has been bitter for a long time change?

What Is Bitterness?

Webster defines *bitter* as "sour, sharp, harsh, sarcastic, hurtful, and stinging." Bitterness can result from a single incident, but it usually develops over time. Bitterness is an attitude of the heart affecting the entire person.

Bitterness springs from a root of resentment. The Christian is cautioned to "exercise foresight and be on the watch to look [after one another], to see that no one falls back from and fails to secure God's grace . . . in order that no root of resentment (rancor, bitterness, or hatred) shoots forth and causes trouble and bitter torment, and the many become contaminated and defiled by it—" (Hebrews 12:15). If it is not confronted and resolved, anger leads to resentment. Unresolved resentment leads to a pervasive attitude of bitterness.

The results of bitterness are many. Bitterness causes "trouble and bitter torment." Some of the troubles bitterness causes include jealousy, dissension, immorality (Hebrews 12:14–17), confusion (James 3:14–16), and illness (Proverbs 14:30). The attitude of a bitter person *affects* and *infects* many.

Some years ago, I met a physician who asked me to see a lady who had numerous complaints, but no physical cause could be determined. He mentioned that she seemed to have a significant amount of hostility toward a sister. Would I see if I could help her?

Entering the room, I expected to see a relatively young woman. Instead, I was surprised to see a woman in her seventies, tight-lipped and grim. Before I could introduce myself, she had begun listing a series of complaints about the medical care.

When I asked her about her life, she began relating a tale of extreme jealousy toward her sister. This sister had always had everything she herself wanted. Her sister had dated the men she liked and had even married the man she had hoped to win. On and on she talked, pouring out her list of complaints about her sister and about God. God had not been fair to her; He had ignored her and favored her sister instead.

Her anger toward her sister and her bitterness toward God were palpable. When asked whether or not she had any current contact with her sister, she replied, "Oh, heavens no! She's been dead for twenty years now!"

This woman had continued to affect and infect others with her bitterness twenty years after the source of her bitterness had died. This woman had missed most of what life had to offer because of her bitterness!

God's Solution for Bitterness

God has a sure plan for bitterness; His Word is clear on the dangers bitterness presents to a person. Your friend needs to hear what God says.

Forgiveness

Forgiveness is God's plan for dealing with bitterness toward others, because forgiveness deals a death-blow to resentment and bitterness.

The Christian should "Let all bitterness and indignation and wrath (passion, rage, bad temper) and resentment (anger, animosity) and quarreling (brawling, clamor, contention) and slander (evil-speaking, abusive or blasphemous language) be banished from you, with all malice (spite, ill will, or baseness of any kind). And become useful and helpful and kind to one another, tenderhearted (compassionate, understanding, loving-hearted), *forgiving one another* [*readily and freely*], *as God in Christ forgave you*" (Ephesians 4:31–32, emphasis added).

Although forgiveness is the key that unlocks the chains of bitterness, forgiving is difficult for a person who is bitter. You may find that when you begin to talk to your bitter friend about her need to forgive, you will meet with resistance. Even if she is willing to forgive, she may be unable to do so because of her misconceptions about forgiveness.

Your friend may believe that as long as she doesn't forgive, she will not be vulnerable to the person who hurt her—that somehow *unforgiveness protects her*. But refusing to forgive does not protect a person; unforgiveness destroys. Forgiveness has nothing to do with protection. Your friend may be hurt again, whether or not she has forgiven. If she hasn't forgiven, however, her unforgiveness is sure to hurt her!

Your friend may also believe that if she forgives, she is *condoning* the wrong behavior. Forgiving or pardoning an offender is not the same as condoning an offense.

Forgiveness does not change the fact that an offense occurred. Forgiveness does, however, free the one who was offended from the offender.

Another misconception your friend may have is that if she forgives, she will then have to *act as though the offense never occurred*. Giving up the attitude of bitterness and choosing to forgive does not mean that she must have a close relationship with the person who has offended her, nor does it mean she must spend time with her offender, or even enjoy this person. It does not mean that your friend has to live as if she were never wounded. Forgiveness means only that she pardons, lets go of the resentment, and decides to give up wishing harm or punishment toward that person.

Some are resistant to forgiving because of pride. Sometimes withholding forgiveness from another simply involves the pride of being right.

Bonnie was an attractive woman in her early thirties who had come for counseling because of problems associated with childhood sexual abuse. Her father had left her family when she was a baby, and she had been sexually abused by her stepfather. She grew up thinking that her natural father was cruel and uncaring and that if he hadn't left her, she wouldn't have been abused. After a period of time, she had been able to forgive her stepfather for the abuse, as well as her mother for not protecting her.

"Many pay a high price to be right. Pride-breaking is painful but thankfully brief!"

When I next saw her, however, she was again struggling with the problem of unforgiveness. She had recently come into contact with members of her father's family. They told her how much like her father she was and that her father had attempted to contact her through the years before his death. Her mother, however, had refused to allow him to see her.

"I know I should be happy that he tried to contact me and that he must have cared," she exclaimed, "but I feel so angry! Why didn't they tell me this before? I can't change the way I feel toward him now! It's too late! I *know* he didn't really care!"

177

Many pay a high price to be right. Pride-breaking is painful but thankfully brief! The results are a clear conscience before God and freedom from the pain of unforgiveness and bitterness.

Some let pride keep them from forgiving, but others are reluctant to give up the role of victim. Your friend may have been the victim for so many years that it is like a second skin. She may see herself as the wronged party, the mistreated victim. However, forgiveness means giving up the role of the victim.

One woman had been an inpatient in the psychiatric unit of the local hospital at least once a year for the past five years. After two years without hospitalization, she commented, "Sometimes I miss being crazy because I got so much attention."

A victim often receives sympathy and attention, but she confuses this with love. You must help your friend understand that sympathy and attention are not the same as love. In relinquishing the victim role, she can receive real love.

The results of holding on to bitterness are devastating. Forgiveness is a small price to pay for freedom!

Surrender

While forgiveness is God's solution for those who are bitter toward others, trusting surrender is His answer for those who are bitter toward Him.

Job was a man who was in danger of bitterness toward God. The Bible tells us he was an upright man who feared God and abstained from evil (Job 1:1). When Job lost his family, possessions, and health, he couldn't understand why God had allowed this to happen to him. His friends offered counsel, saying he must have committed some sin for all of this calamity to have fallen on him. In the midst of his trouble, Job asked God "Why?" but received no answer.

178

Another friend told him it was because he wasn't listening. Finally Job cried, "It profits a man nothing that he should delight himself with God and consent to Him" (Job 34:9). This was Job's bitter moment toward God.

When Job seemed at his lowest point, God intervened. Instead of answering Job's question of "Why?" however, He showed him His power and sovereignty over the earth. He told Job that if Job couldn't create or understand the physical world, how could he understand the mind of God?

Job's response was to surrender to the majesty and power of God. Job declared, "I know that You can do all things, and that no thought or purpose of Yours can be restrained or thwarted.

"When Job seemed at his lowest point, God intervened."

"[You said to me] Who is this that darkens and obscures counsel [by words] without knowledge? Therefore [I now see] I have [rashly] uttered what I did not understand, things too wonderful for me, which I did not know" (Job 42:2–3). His surrender to the sovereignty of God brought him release from bitterness.

Resentment and bitterness toward God will prevent your friend from receiving His love and knowing Him as gentle Father. Only in complete surrender to God will your friend find rest. The person who is afraid of surrender to God doesn't understand His love. Your friend must believe these words:

There is no fear in love [dread does not exist], but full-grown (complete, perfect) love turns fear out of doors and expels every trace of terror! For fear brings with it the thought of punishment, and [so] he who is afraid has not reached the full maturity of love [is not yet grown into love's complete perfection]. (1 John 4:18)

Refilling

When we let go of bitterness through acts of forgiveness and surrender, we need to let God fill the space the bitterness occupied with Himself. This "refilling" is God's third solution for the bitterness problem.

The need is for us to be "filled [through all your being] unto all the fullness of God [may have the richest measure of the divine Presence, and become a body wholly filled and flooded with God Himself]!" (Ephesians 3:19).

When we are refilled with God's Holy Spirit, instead of bitterness, we exhibit the fruits of the Spirit—love, joy, peace, patience, kindness, goodness, faithfulness, gentleness, and self-control (Galatians 5:22–23).

When we are filled with the love of God, a sense of His presence, His peace, His joy, His power, and His strength leaves no room for a root of resentment or bitterness to fester and grow.

Ways to Help

When your friend realizes the root of bitterness in her life, she will need your guidance in freeing herself from its grip.

Steps of Forgiveness

First, help your friend recognize that forgiveness is a choice. Remind her that forgiveness has nothing to do with feeling. In fact, she will probably never *feel like* forgiving!

Forgiveness is an act of the will. Her part is to be willing to forgive; God's part is to complete the transaction in her heart.

It might be helpful for you to share a personal experience of forgiveness with her, emphasizing the idea of choice.

Second, help your friend identify the offenses. Doing this will help your friend to clarify exactly what resentments she is releasing. I have found it helpful to have people make lists of persons and offenses. I also ask them to write beside each offense when it happened and the number of years since that time. For example, see chart below.

A Offenses	B Year committed	C Number of years that have passed
He humiliated me in front of my friends	1951	40 years

This will give your friend a clear picture of the specific

offenses, and how long she has held the resentment and bitterness.

Third, discuss the advantages of forgiveness with her. Remind your friend that she is the one who will benefit from forgiving her offender.

Fourth, pray with her to forgive. I have found it helpful to go through her list, saying for each item, "In the name of Jesus, I choose to forgive _____ for _____." If she is uncomfortable doing this with you, suggest that she do it alone. It is important, however, for her to say aloud her decision to forgive. This helps to imprint the decision in her mind and in her heart.

Fifth, take some type of action. After your friend has gone through each item on her list, have her tear up the list or do something else to symbolically release her bitterness. Another thing you might suggest is that she burn the list. One woman threw her list into the Arkansas River!

Sixth, mark the occasion. Have your friend do something to mark the occasion. In the Old Testament, the children of Israel made rock altars to commemorate events. She might want to buy something, such as a piece of jewelry, as a reminder of her act of forgiveness. She might want to take a hot bubble bath, symbolizing the cleansing of her heart. Or she might want to share her experience with another friend who will rejoice with her.

Steps of Surrender

The first step in surrender is admitting to God and to another person the sin of bitterness. Help your friend confess to God her lack of trust in Him and the reasons for her bitterness.

Second, have your friend ask God to forgive her for her bitterness and any specific actions which have resulted from this attitude. Often a person will gossip, leave a church, or quit spending time with God, all due to bitterness. If your friend has acted out her bitterness in any way, help her to confess this and to ask God for His forgiveness.

Third, help your friend to find Scripture verses that speak to her needs. It is common for people to become bitter, thinking that God has failed them in some way. If this is the case, help your friend to see the ways God has provided for her, and find Scripture verses that describe His provision and grace.

Fourth, help your friend to identify any areas of her life in which she has not completely surrendered to God.

Finally, lead her in a prayer of surrender in these areas. Have her tell God that she wants His will in the _____ area of her life, that she entrusts herself to Him. It is sometimes helpful to write on separate pieces of paper the areas of surrender; then in whatever manner is meaningful to her, she can offer them to God. This helps give your friend a picture of her act of surrender.

Steps in Refilling

After your friend has released her bitterness through forgiveness and surrendered herself to the Father, pray with her to be refilled by the Holy Spirit. You might want to pray a Scripture passage such as Ephesians 3:16–21 or ask God to fill her with the fruits of the Spirit found in Galatians 5. God always answers our prayers to be filled up with His love and with Himself.

Assure your friend that her transaction has been recorded in heaven. God has heard her prayer, and He has intervened. Following her decision to forgive, He will complete the work in her emotions.

Rejoice with your friend for what God has done. Praise

is a deterrent to bitterness! Encourage her to keep a note-book of daily praise and thanksgiving.

> Through Him, therefore, let us constantly and at all times offer up to God a sacrifice of praise, which is the fruit of lips that thankfully acknowledge and confess and glorify His name. (Hebrews 13:15)

LIFE APPLICATIONS

1. Share a time when you felt resentment and bitterness toward another person. How did you feel physically? Emotionally? Spiritually?

2. Have you ever known someone who refused to forgive another person? What was that person like? Were you drawn toward that person?

3. How were you able to let go of the bitterness? What did you do? What were the results?

4. Have you ever heard anyone say, "Forgive and forget"? Do you think you can forgive without forgetting? Why or why not?

5. Have you ever felt bitter toward God? This chapter says that "trusting surrender" is God's answer for bitterness against Him. Why do you believe this is true or not true?

6. Why do you think it is important to be "refilled" by God after episodes of bitterness and surrender? Can you recall a time in which He refilled you?

7. Is there anyone you need to forgive? Will you take that action? Is there any restitution you need to make?

8. What is something you could do to symbolize your spiritual transaction of forgiveness?

12

GUILT

Because of my sins, I am bent and wracked with
pain. My days are filled with anguish.
PSALM 38:6

I feel guilty about everything. When something goes
wrong, I feel as if it's my fault. It's hard for me to believe
God really loves me!"

Have you had a friend who felt like this? Guilt is a major hindrance to experiencing God's love and growing close
to Him. When we feel guilty, we are hesitant to ask God for
help or for blessing. Shame, fear, and doubt are our constant companions.

Guilt, like any emotion, can be helpful *or* harmful. The
guilt we feel when we have sinned can be beneficial if we
allow it to cause us to repent and change. Guilt that is not
faced, or false guilt that is placed on us by another person,
however, can be damaging, leading to feelings of worthless-
ness and shame.

Guilt has many facets. How can you help a friend understand the difference between true and false guilt? How
can she get rid of guilt and shame? How can she be free
from the guilt of the past?

187

True Guilt, False Guilt, or Regret?

Does God cause us to feel guilty to punish us for our sins? Does He use guilt to control our behavior? Unfortunately, these beliefs are common among those from "Christian" homes in which the wrath of God and withdrawal of love were used to enforce obedience.

True Guilt

Guilt is not a punishment, but a blessing! True guilt, the kind that occurs when we have done something wrong, is the only kind of guilt God wants His children to experience. Why?

> . . . so that *in nothing you might suffer loss* . . . For godly grief and the pain God is permitted to direct, produce a repentance that leads and contributes to salvation and deliverance from evil, and *it never brings regret.* (2 Corinthians 7:9–10, emphasis added)

If you have a friend who is denying or avoiding her sins, she will pay a high price indeed.

Sandy came for counseling two years after the death of her husband, Thomas. She explained that six months ago she had met Richard, a fine Christian man in her church. Then, with tears forming in her eyes, she said, "I really love him, and he really loves me, but I'm so afraid to marry him! I can't tell him yes, but I can't tell him no. I'm so confused! Can you help me?"

Over the next few weeks, Sandy revealed she and Thomas had married impulsively and against her parents' wishes as soon as they had graduated from high school. When problems arose early in their young marriage, Sandy determined to prove her parents wrong, working very hard to make her marriage succeed. As time went on, however, she became disheartened and filled with disappointment.

As the years passed, Sandy found her loneliness unbearable, and she began an affair with a man in her neighborhood. She knew her involvement with this man was wrong, but she couldn't seem to stop herself. She was too ashamed to tell anyone and felt too guilty to continue attending their local church.

"True guilt, the kind that occurs when we have done something wrong, is the only kind of guilt God wants His children to experience."

A year after the affair began, Thomas arrived home early one evening, sobbing. Sandy was petrified. Had he found out about her affair? Instead of the accusation she expected, however, Thomas cried, "Honey! I'm sick! I saw a doctor last week, and he ran some tests. I saw him again today, and he said that I have cancer!" His face white, he continued, "He said there's nothing they can do! I only have a few months! What are we going to do?"

Shame and guilt flooded over Sandy. "How could he have become this sick without my realizing?" she accused herself. Remembering how engrossed she had been in her affair for the past year, she felt thoughts darting at her from all directions. "If I hadn't been having an affair, maybe Thomas wouldn't have gotten sick! I might have noticed! I can't remember the last time I even looked at him. I've been so wrapped up in myself! What kind of a monster have I become?"

Immediately ending her adulterous relationship, Sandy devoted herself to making Thomas's last months as comfortable as possible. She stayed at the hospital from dawn until late at night, almost destroying her own health in her efforts to atone for her infidelity to Thomas. Thomas's family remarked often, "Sandy can't do enough for him. What a good wife she is!"

When Thomas finally died, it seemed that Sandy's grief was endless. For months, she refused to see her friends and rarely left home. Finally, one year after Thomas's death, she went to work. It was during that time she met Richard, the man with whom she had fallen in love.

Although Sandy had stopped her affair, she had never acknowledged her sin to God and received His cleansing and forgiveness. Instead, she had tried to atone for her sin through a self-imposed penance and continued fear and shame. She had kept her guilt, and it had imprisoned her! She felt she didn't deserve happiness with Richard, and she feared that he would be unfaithful to her as she had been unfaithful to Thomas.

False Guilt

Sandy's guilt was a consequence of her own sin, but many have been made to feel guilty for the sins and mistakes of others. When people carry guilt for others, they become victims of false guilt. False guilt occurs when we have not actually done something wrong, but we have been led to believe that we have.

I was the first and only child of my parents, born after eighteen childless years of marriage. Although I have happy memories of my childhood, from a very early age I felt a sense of responsibility for the happiness of my parents.

I didn't understand it at the time, but it was as though there was a "warning" hovering over my life, reminding me that I mustn't do or say anything that would upset Mother.

When I left home to attend college, my mother had a recurrence of the depression and anxiety which she had suffered as a young adult. Her condition worsened as, during the following year, my fiancé, Wayne, and I began to make plans for our wedding. The month before we were married, she had to be hospitalized and was unable to attend the wedding. I felt so guilty for my own happiness when Mother was so unhappy! My guilt increased when, soon after our marriage, my father became seriously ill and died.

Mother's depression worsened, and I spent the early years of my marriage trying to help her, in addition to settling in a home and taking care of two young sons. Mother's depression began to be expressed toward me in anger. She would say to me, "You have everything! A husband, a home, and children! I have no one to take care of me!" I began to think that I should never have left home, that I should have stayed. Then maybe none of this would have happened!

The guilt that I felt from my mother made it almost impossible for me to enjoy being a wife and mother. I didn't realize then that I was the victim of false guilt.

Because false guilt and real guilt *feel* alike, some may go for years without knowing the difference. False guilt is placed on someone either to control, to exact revenge, or to avoid one's own guilt.

Regret

It is easy for many to mistake sorrow that results from a mistake for true guilt. There is a difference, however, between guilt and regret.

"I'll never get over what I've done!" Patsy told me.

"Every night I wake up reliving the accident. I can still hear the screech of the tires and the screams of the people. I can't believe I didn't see the stop sign or the car coming! How can I ever live with what I've done! I wish I had died instead of that young mother!"

Guilt results from a sin—a deliberate action. Regret, on the other hand, may result from a mistake—an action taken out of ignorance or carelessness. Patsy's overwhelming feelings of sorrow were identical to those she would have felt if she had deliberately murdered someone. She made a mistake that had terrible consequences, but she had not deliberately sinned. It took Patsy many months to understand the difference between causing someone's death by carelessness and the deliberate, premeditated sin of murder. She needed healing and release from sorrow as well as help in living with the consequences of her mistake. She didn't need forgiveness of sin.

Characteristics of the Guilty

Whether your friend is burdened by true guilt or false guilt, there are some characteristics common to both. If you observe several of these characteristics, it is probable your friend needs help in resolving guilt or experiencing forgiveness.

Self-condemnation

If your friend has not faced her guilt and received God's forgiveness, she will tend to condemn herself. Thinking that someone must pay for what she has done, she may punish herself through self-destructive behaviors, such as sabotaging blessings or setting up rejection. Although she may be conscious of doing so, usually people are not always aware of why they treat themselves harshly.

Sandy's feeling that she didn't deserve a man like Richard is a good example of self-condemnation. She was unable to receive Richard's love, because she had condemned herself to a life without hope of another marriage.

A Need for Penance

When Sandy almost ruined her health before Thomas died, her efforts were not motivated by a love for Thomas but were actually an effort to atone for her own sins. But, no matter how self-sacrificing she had been to her dying husband, she could not rid herself of guilt, nor could she find peace regarding her future after his death.

You may have a friend who mistakenly believes, consciously or unconsciously, that if she suffers "enough" she will be released from her guilt. Unfortunately, no amount of penance can cleanse the soul. Only God, through Jesus, can accomplish that.

Many Fears

Guilty people entertain many fears. If your friend fears she will get what she deserves, her confidence about the future will be extremely limited. She will have difficulty trusting others, because she knows that *she* has not been trustworthy, and *she* has not been forgiven.

When Sandy said, "I'm afraid that someday he'll be unfaithful to me!" she was projecting her own guilt onto Richard, fearing that *he* would do to *her* what *she* had done to Thomas. Her guilt had translated itself into fear.

Supersensitivity

If your friend is guilty, she may be supervigilant and supersensitive to the comments of others. She may tend to interpret comments made to her as having hidden meanings.

For example, a perfectly innocent question such as

"What have you been doing today?" may trigger in a guilty person doubts such as "What do they know? Have I been caught? What did she mean by that?"

Blame and Rationalization

You may observe evidence of blameshifting. "But I only did it because . . ." This is exactly what Adam did when he blamed Eve for his sin and what Eve did in blaming the serpent. It's an old lie.

When we sin, it is tempting to rationalize or to blame someone else. "I didn't really intend to do that. I was just so lonely." Or "Everyone else does things like that. Don't I have the right to a little happiness?"

Listen to your friend. Does she justify her behavior with "good excuses"? Does she blame someone else for her choices? If she refuses to accept responsibility for her own behavior, her guilt can never be faced or released.

Shame and Fear of Exposure

Have you ever done something wrong, and although you felt guilty, you were nevertheless confident that no one knew? Was your action later exposed? If so, can you remember the embarrassment you felt? When exposure occurs, shame floods our hearts. It brings many fears—fear of gossip or ridicule, loss of position, family, job, or respect of others, and, of course, the loss of self-respect.

Shame is a terrible price to pay for unconfessed sin. And it is so unnecessary.

Betty was a young woman who managed petty cash in her office. Because of financial burdens, she began to "borrow" from the fund at the end of each week. Soon she began to feel guilty, so she started paying back the amount she had taken. One day, however, her supervisor realized that money was missing, and she confronted Betty with her suspicions. Although Betty had taken responsibility for her actions and had begun replacing the money, her face flooded red with embarrassment, and she felt ashamed. Her sin had been discovered, and she wanted to hide.

Betty's reaction was similar to Adam and Eve's when they covered themselves with fig leaves and hid themselves from God. When we are caught in our sins, we experience a tremendous desire to hide. We feel compelled to hide from others, and we feel inclined to hide from God.

Depression

Whether the guilt is true guilt or false guilt, if your friend feels a need to hide from others or God, she will also experience depression. Because she must expend a great deal of energy just to keep from facing the problem or allowing it to surface, emotional as well as physical and spiritual strength will be sapped.

At this point, you may find your friend withdrawing and avoiding friends, church activities, and other usually enjoyable contacts.

There is nothing your friend can do on her own to cleanse herself from her sin—including self-condemnation, penance, blame, rationalization, justification, or avoidance. Miserable people are those who have not received God's forgiveness for their sins.

Ways to Help

How you help depends on whether your friend is experiencing false guilt or true guilt. The emotional pain will be the same for both; gaining freedom from each will require your friend to face the truth of her situation.

If Your Friend Is Experiencing False Guilt

You might ask her some of the following questions:

- "Exactly what did *you* do that was wrong?"
- "Did someone blame you for what happened?"
- "Did you know that what you were doing was wrong?"
- "Were you really at fault?"
- "Why might you have been the object of accusation?"

If you and your friend determine that she is experiencing false guilt, pray together that God will remove the burden of guilt and shame, as well as the accompanying feelings.

Often, when people realize they have borne guilt imposed upon them by someone else, much anger toward that person will surface. In order for your friend to be free from the past, you will need to help her face her anger squarely and forgive the person who laid the false guilt upon her. To help her through this process, you may want to refer to chapters 6: "Anger," and 11: "Bitterness."

Remind your friend that she does not need to repent because of false guilt. You need to help her to recognize that she is innocent. She must declare herself free and forgive the one who imprisoned her!

If Your Friend Is Experiencing True Guilt

If your friend is experiencing true guilt, and she has not received God's forgiveness, how can you help? How can you help her to face the knowledge of her sin? Can she expect God's help to live with the consequences of what she has done? If her sin has been discovered, how can you help her deal with her feelings of shame and embarrassment? Is there any way for her to feel clean again? Is there a way to go on, to expect life to be good again, regardless of what has been done?

Lovingly Listen

Pray for an opportunity as well as an ability to lovingly listen to your friend. Confession does not come easily, especially if guilt and shame have plagued your friend for a long time. Listen carefully for defensiveness or pride. Approach the subject of pride gently, reminding her that it is painful when pride breaks, but afterward she will experience peace which will be worth the pain. You might remind her, "It's worth it to be free." Or "I understand how you feel. I remember how hard it was for me."

God's Word promises her that "The Lord is close to those who are of a broken heart and saves such as are crushed with sorrow for sin and are humbly and thoroughly penitent" (Psalm 34:18).

Be Open

With discretion, be open about your own past sins, and consider sharing a personal failure. Be prayerful about this, however, because you need to know that you can trust your friend to keep your confidence, just as you will keep hers. Consider whether the details are either necessary or edifying.

If you do not feel it is wise to share a specific, personal experience, let her know you can identify with her feelings, if not the exact situation. Tell her you will not judge or condemn her, because you have also needed God's forgiveness.

Explain the Need for Confession and Repentance

The book of James reminds us to "Confess to one another therefore your faults (your slips, your false steps, your offenses, your sins) and pray [also] for one another, that you may be healed and restored [to a spiritual tone of mind and heart]" (James 5:16). Confession, although never easy, is helpful because then we can no longer hide our "secret." Secret sins exert a fearsome force. When a secret sin is confessed to another person, it loses its power.

Confession is also valuable because it deals a deathblow to our pride. After confession, we can never again misrepresent ourselves as something we are not. We have renounced our claim to any degree of self-righteousness. It is then that we can truly relax, accept our humble position in God's kingdom, and leave the past behind.

Feeling forgiven is a problem for many. Confession not only dissolves the power of secret sins and deals a deathblow to our pride, but confession also helps us feel cleansed.

Joseph said to me, "I confessed my sin to God and completely turned away from it, but thoughts of what I had done continued to bother me. Finally, I confessed my actions to an elder in my church. Although I had a tremendous need to tell someone, it was a scary thing to do! I had no idea what his response would be, but he was very kind. He prayed that I would be free from recurring thoughts about my sin, and since then, my mind has been free!"

Encourage your friend to confess her sins, not only to God, but also to another person. Help her to prayerfully consider in whom she should confide. Assure her that she does not need to give specific details, such as names or places, but she does need to confess what she has done. Remind her of the words of David:

I acknowledged my sin to You, and my iniquity I did not hide. I said, I will confess my transgressions to the Lord [continually unfolding the past till all is told]—then you [instantly] forgave me the guilt and iniquity of my sin. (Psalm 32:5)

If she wants to confess to you, assure her that you will keep confidential all she tells you. It is sometimes helpful to ask her to read aloud Psalm 51:1–7. God's Word will add validity and power to her confession.

After your friend has confessed, if you feel led to do so, pray with her, asking God to deliver and heal her of the effects of her sin, as well as the guilt and shame of it. Thank God for His mercy and love for her. Before you conclude praying, promise God that you will never repeat the information which your friend has given to you. This will assure her of your confidentiality, and it will impress upon you that you are accountable to God.

If she has expressed fear that her sin will later be "found out," remind her of David's words: "You are a hiding place for me; You, Lord, preserve me from trouble, You surround me with songs and shouts of deliverance" (Psalm 32:7). If she is afraid of those whom she has harmed in the past, remind her that "When a man's ways please the Lord, He makes even his enemies to be at peace with him" (Proverbs 16:7).

Confession, however, is not complete without repentance or change: "So repent (change your mind and purpose); turn around and return [to God], that your sins may be erased (blotted out, wiped clean), that times of refreshing (of recovering from the effects of heat, of reviving with fresh air) may come from the presence of the Lord" (Acts 3:19).

Talk with your friend about the difference between simply being sorry for a sin—wanting relief from its pain—and turning from the sin once and for all. Confession without repentance brings only temporary relief. Confession *and* repentance bring the refreshing and reviving power and presence of God!

Look at the Issue of Penance

If your friend has been doing penance, trying to compensate for her sin, explain how unnecessary her action is. Remind her that God does not want her sacrifice, but He wants her to know and love Him (Hosea 6:6). He does not require penance, but He requires her confession and repentance, in order that she might be cleansed and receive His blessings.

"Confession and repentance bring the refreshing and reviving power and presence of God!"

Make a Plan

As your friendship grows, help your friend gain all that she can from past sins and mistakes. To protect her in the future, help her to identify her points of vulnerability which left her open to temptation in the past. Ask her to confide in you if she becomes tempted to commit the same sin again.

Encourage Her to Obey

If your friend feels that God has asked her to make restitution for her past actions in some way, help her evaluate her intentions carefully. Ascertain that she is not falling into an old trap of penance. If she desires genuinely to restore damage which she has caused, and if it appears that her actions would indeed heal a situation, encourage her to do so.

Get Involved with Other Christians

Invite your friend to attend church again. Encourage her participation in small groups which will provide the type of support that she needs. Receiving love and encouragement from others will overcome the sense of isolation and unworthiness she has felt.

Mark the Occasion

You may consider giving your friend a symbol of her new freedom, such as a cross, a flower, a charm, a book, or something else special. This can serve as a visual reminder of her release from guilt.

Freedom from Guilt

Guilt is an insidious and destructive state. Because Jesus died on the Cross for our sins, we are able to come freely to the throne of God without any fear (Hebrews 4:16). We can know that God has thoroughly cleansed us from our sin and guilt (1 John 1:9). We can ask for what we need without any hesitation (1 John 5:14). And we can begin to live the life that He laid out for us before the foundation of the world (Ephesians 1:4). Freedom from guilt is truly a gift of our loving Father!

LIFE APPLICATIONS _____

1. Can you relate a time when you experienced false guilt? Why do you think your guilt was "false"?

2. Can you agree that true guilt is a blessing? Why?

3. Have you ever confused guilt and regret? How?

4. Has there been a time in your life when you have postponed dealing with a sin? Did your body "speak to you" about this? If so, what were your symptoms?

5. Have you ever been blamed for something that was definitely not your fault? How did you react?

6. Why is it important, in some situations, to confess your sin to another person? Have you ever done this? What happened?

7. Have you ever wronged someone and later received their complete forgiveness? How did you feel?

8. Have you ever blamed someone for something that was really your fault? Did your pride prevent you from taking responsibility for your actions?

9. Read Hebrews 4:16.

13

SELF-ESTEEM

I have been crucified with Christ; . . . it is no longer I
who live, but Christ (the Messiah) lives in me.

GALATIANS 2:20

I'm worried about my daughter. She seems depressed.
I'm afraid she has low self-esteem."

"I don't like myself. I can't seem to accomplish all that
others do. My self-esteem is really low!"

"My husband doesn't seem to really care about other
people. Is that because he doesn't know how to love himself?"

Self-esteem is a term used in recent years. Both the sec-
ular world and, more recently, the Christian church have
concerned themselves with improving self-esteem. A great
deal of money has been spent on books, seminars, tapes,
conferences, and therapy devoted to this topic. But what is
self-esteem? How do you help a friend increase personal
self-esteem? What is the key to loving yourself and others?

Self-esteem is a confusing term, which some in Christian circles have opposed on the grounds that self-*esteem*
means self-*worship*. Others have reduced it to merely liking
oneself. Whatever the actual meaning of the word, most

people use self-esteem to refer to their perception of themselves. Whether or not one has "high self-esteem" or "low self-esteem" appears to have great influence upon whether or not one will be loved, successful, confident, secure, approved of, or feel worthwhile. With conflicting definitions of the very term, there is even more confusion as to how a person can attain greater self-esteem.

Unfortunately, Satan perverts what God desires for His children. In many self-esteem doctrines, *self* has become the center focus. Because of this, the desire to "feel good about myself" has led many into a subtle deception.

The Deception

In May 1975, I was sitting in a training class on "How to Increase Your Self-esteem." As I glanced around the room, I noticed that many in attendance were women in their late twenties and mid-thirties. Since the women's liberation movement had gathered force, many women were entering the career world for the first time. There was an air of excitement and adventure in the room.

The speaker, a stylishly dressed professional woman, commanded our attention immediately when she asked, "Do you like yourself? Do people often intimidate you? Do you know how to take charge of a difficult situation? Do you know that you are important? Do you have a high level of self-esteem?"

She continued, "If you are going to be successful in the world today, it is important that you know *who* you are and *where* you are going. You *must* like yourself, or you will *never* be a confident person. Do you feel comfortable standing up for yourself? Asserting your rights? You have to learn to do for *yourself*, to put yourself *first*, and to be on your *own side!* You are the best friend you will ever have. If you don't like yourself and take care of yourself, *no one else will do it for you!"*

Her words stunned me. They didn't sound like anything I had ever heard before. I had not really thought much about how I felt about myself. I could recall having had twinges of self-consciousness or inferiority, and I had compared myself to other women; but usually I was content to enthusiastically do the work I believed God had called me to do. Now, all of a sudden, my *self* became the center of my attention. Did I have good self-esteem? What *did* I think about myself? I leaned forward and listened carefully.

"Whatever the actual meaning of the word, most people use self-esteem to refer to their perception of themselves."

"Write down all of the positive characteristics about yourself that you can," she continued. We all glanced around the room at each other, laughing nervously in response to the assignment. On one hand, I was hoping that I could think of enough positive things to make a list. On the other hand, I was hoping that I would remain modest, in case someone else saw my lengthy list of goodness and lose whatever self-esteem she might have!

"Now write down every accomplishment you have made since the first of this year." Then, we were advised to continue making such lists throughout the year, carefully recording our personal improvements, as well as our accomplishments. With the assurance that as our lists grew, we would feel better and better about ourselves, the morning session ended.

By the end of that day, I was on my way to becoming a different person. In the months that followed, I began to strive to find ways to improve my self-esteem. I was driven to do more and more so that I could prove that I was a worthwhile, capable person. I became competitive, not only with others, but with myself. The more I wanted to accomplish, the less my fulfillment came from helping people. I became focused on my personal success. When I was more productive, my self-esteem rose; however, when my striving did not produce the desired results, my self-esteem fell. As time went on, I began to wonder if perhaps I had only added a very complicated dimension to my former simple lifestyle.

Why didn't I like myself more? Why wasn't I *happy?* I was actually beginning to like myself less! I was tired! More and greater accomplishments were needed to keep me feeling good about myself. As my misery increased, God began to give me a glimmer of understanding about the mistake I had made. *I had begun to live for myself.* I had become a restless, striving person who had lost peace of mind, as well as a clear sense of purpose.

Does this sound familiar? Is your friend's self-esteem "high" or "low"? Is she striving? Does she feel unworthy, insecure? Is she trying to *earn* admiration, believing that admiration results in being loved? If so, she may believe the deception!

The deception of the self-esteem movement is that we base our identities on who we are, what we have done, whom we know, how much money we make, how many possessions we own, how many degrees we have, what we have achieved. We have been deceived into thinking that we can feel good about ourselves through our own *self-effort.*

But we never completely measure up. When we reach the goal set for ourselves, we find that we still don't feel loved or worthy. We have learned that while our achievements, fame, reputation, or our status have made us feel good, the pleasure is short-lived. We have learned that these don't touch the core of our being—the real person inside who just wants to be loved and accepted for who we are, not what we can do.

"The way to wholeness comes from having a right relationship with our Father, knowing how He sees us, and loving Him and others."

Being admired will not guarantee that we will be loved; it may simply cause us to be envied. Others may respect us or be in awe of us, but they may not necessarily be drawn to us. In fact, we may simply cause them to remain at a distance.

"Feeling good about myself" is a cheap imitation of the peace of God. Happiness due only to success may feel similar to the joy of the Holy Spirit, but it is unstable because it depends entirely upon circumstances. "Taking charge of my life" is not equal to the self-control described as a fruit of the Holy Spirit (Galatians 5:22–23).

The deception many have believed is that self-esteem

comes from achievement, success, knowledge, status, beauty, possessions, position, or personality.

The Way to Wholeness

The way to wholeness comes from having a right relationship with our Father, knowing how He sees us, and loving Him and others.

A counselor confided, "One of the underlying reasons I studied psychology was to discover how to feel better about myself. I had the mistaken idea God was a person I had to please by obeying a set of rules which I couldn't keep, in spite of my best efforts. If the answer wasn't in God, then it must lie somewhere within myself. I was confident that my study of psychology would help me find the truth.

"After obtaining my master's degree; achieving promotions and honors in my work; having good friends and material possessions—I realized my self-esteem was still low. I had everything that should make me happy on the outside, but inside I was lonely, insecure, unhappy, and dissatisfied. I wasn't at peace, nor did I have true joy. I felt that something was missing.

"At this point, I began to look again to God. I began to realize that God loved me, that Jesus was alive and available to me in a personal way, and that the Holy Spirit was the One who would give me the power to love and obey. My life totally changed. Gradually, I began to truly realize the love of God in my life, and I found I was able to really love others. Problems that had bothered me for years began to be healed as I got to know God as my Father. For the first time in my life, I felt solid . . . truly loved, secure, free!"

Only knowing God and experiencing His love can cause us to feel secure. The shed blood of Jesus grants us security now and forever. God's grace gives divine approval.

We cannot build our own self-esteem; it must come from God. Only through a relationship with our Father and in knowing we are loved, forgiven, and accepted in spite of what we have or have not done can we find the way to wholeness.

A Right Relationship with God

One woman related, "Growing up in a church, I had always heard that Jesus had died on the Cross to pay for my sins. Yet somehow I had the idea that *I* had to be good enough to pay for my sins and earn a right relationship with God. But I found that no matter how hard I tried, I couldn't be good enough to be acceptable to God."

"We cannot build our own self-esteem; it must come from God."

The Bible says that the penalty for sin is death (Romans 6:23). But God made a way whereby man could have a right relationship with Him without having to die. He sent His Son, Jesus, to die in our place:

> [All] are justified and made upright and in right standing with God, freely and gratuitously by His grace (His un-merited favor and mercy), through the redemption which is [provided] in Christ Jesus. (Romans 3:24)

As you work with your friend who has low self-esteem, first help her realize that only through accepting Jesus as her Savior and Lord can she have a right standing with God the Father. In Him, all of the sins she has ever committed are forgiven. God the Father then sees her as cleansed, pure, holy—as if she had never sinned. She can then approach God boldly, without fear, knowing she is loved and accepted—no matter what she has been or done (Hebrews 4:16).

What a relief to know that, "Therefore, if any person is [ingrafted] in Christ (the Messiah) he is a new creation (a new creature altogether); the old [previous moral and spiritual condition] has passed away. Behold, the fresh and new has come!" (2 Corinthians 5:17).

Does your friend know Jesus as her Savior and Lord? Has she been forgiven for all of the wrong things she has ever done? Has the Holy Spirit come into her human spirit and given her new birth? Does she feel that she can talk with God personally? Are her prayers answered?

A Clear Conscience

"I just couldn't look Betty in the face," Dorothy confided to her friend Susan. "I felt so bad that I had lied to her. I couldn't sleep or eat until I had told her the truth!"

A guilty conscience is a definite deterrent to self-esteem. When we have a right relationship with God, our consciences are clear because we have confessed our wrongdoings and have been forgiven. We can then approach our Father boldly and confidently "that we may receive mercy [for our failures] and find grace to help in good time for every need [appropriate help and well-timed help, coming just when we need it]" (Hebrews 4:16).

Without a clear conscience, we are unable to accept ourselves, or feel assured of God's blessing.

210

A New Identity

Often Christians have a low self-esteem because they do not realize how God really sees them. They are unaware of the privileges He has freely given them, but instead they see themselves as they were before His Spirit lived in them.

We can take comfort in these words: "For our sake He made Christ [virtually] to be sin Who knew no sin, so that in and through Him we might become [endued with, viewed as being in, and examples of] the righteousness of God [what we ought to be, approved and acceptable and in right relationship with Him, by His goodness]" (2 Corinthians 5:21). Because of Jesus, God sees the believer just like He sees Jesus—wholly acceptable, blameless, and above reproach (Ephesians 1:4).

We become God's own children, adopted into His family, belonging to His own household (Ephesians 2:19), with the privilege of calling Him "Daddy" (Romans 8:15). Because we are in the family, we "are heirs of God and fellow heirs with Christ [sharing His inheritance with Him]" (Romans 8:17; see also Galatians 3:26, 29). We are God's "chosen race, a royal priesthood, a dedicated nation" (1 Peter 2:9).

"I thought when you became a Christian, it just meant you went to heaven when you died," the young man related. "I had no idea that I would have a totally new identity! For the first time in my life, I feel that I have a place, a purpose, and Someone who cares! Why didn't anyone tell me it would be like this?"

The believer is "God's [own] handiwork" (Ephesians 2:10), free from condemnation (Romans 8:1), God's fellow worker (1 Corinthians 3:9), "Christ's ambassadors"

(2 Corinthians 5:20), and the Father sees us as "the sweet fragrance of Christ" (2 Corinthians 2:15).

The believer has available the power of the Holy Spirit, the same power that raised Jesus from the dead (Ephesians 1:19–20; Philippians 4:13). Because of the death of Jesus, we have healing (1 Peter 2:24), protection (Psalm 91), grace and peace (Ephesians 1:2), everything that is needed (Philippians 4:19; Ephesians 1:3), and forgiveness of sins on a daily basis (1 John 1:9).

A Defined Purpose

Each believer has a purpose in God's family. What is it?

> And what does the Lord require of you but to do justly, and to love kindness and mercy, and to humble yourself and walk humbly with your God? (Micah 6:8)

Jesus defined our purpose this way:

> You shall love the Lord your God with all your heart and with all your soul and with all your mind. . . . You shall love your neighbor as [you do] yourself. (Matthew 22:37, 39)

To love God, to walk with Him, and to love others is our highest purpose. This requires no special training or skills; only a willing heart open to God. No matter what your friend's circumstances are in life, God has given her "the ministry of reconciliation [that by word and deed we might aim to bring others into harmony with Him]" (2 Corinthians 5:18).

In order to do this, God promises your friend gifts of His Holy Spirit (see 1 Corinthians 12) which will enable and empower her to serve Him.

I had been seeing the Carr family for several weeks. Most of our sessions had been concerning the behavior of the ten-year-old daughter. On this particular day, I was talking to the mother privately. I felt a strong urge to pray with her. Since I didn't know how she would feel about this, I was somewhat reluctant to ask her permission. The urge, however, became stronger and stronger, until at last I told her what I was feeling. She consented, and I began to pray.

In the midst of my prayer, I was somewhat shocked to hear myself praying, "Father, please let Mrs. Carr know that it hurt You when her stepfather abused her and that You want to heal her." I felt stunned into silence, wondering where the words had come from. Mrs. Carr had never mentioned any type of abuse to me. To my surprise, she began sobbing. "I've never told anyone about the abuse," she cried. "I've always been so ashamed. God really does care, doesn't He?"

This gift of the Spirit, the word of knowledge (1 Corinthians 12:8), and other gifts of the Spirit will be provided by God as they are needed in counseling others. As your friend surrenders to His will, He will show her how to serve and will provide her with what she needs. As your friend grows in her relationship with Jesus, she will experience God's unconditional love for herself, see reproduced in her character the fruits of the Spirit (Galatians 5:22–23), and love and serve others through the anointing of the gifts of the Spirit.

God's Answer to the Self-esteem Problem

God's answer to the self-esteem problem is not to focus on *self*, but to love and serve God and others.

Lose Your Life to Find It

The prevalent self-esteem approaches today focus on how to build up the *self*. But no amount of self-actualization, achievement, or effort can produce a feeling of true security and love. Jesus said, "Whoever finds his [lower] life will lose it [the higher life], and whoever loses his [lower] life on My account will find it [the higher life]" (Matthew 10:39).

The futility of trying to build my sense of self based on my own efforts was graphically and unforgettably illustrated to me one morning as I was praying.

The Holy Spirit spoke plainly, "You are nothing! Without me, you are nothing! Your life is nothing without Me! Nothing! Nothing! Nothing!" According to the self-esteem training I had received, these words should have been crushing to my ego, but they were not. To my surprise, as I let the Words penetrate my mind, I felt the joy of the Holy Spirit rise inside me. For the first time, I understood that I didn't have to try to be *somebody!* I didn't have to be *something!* I didn't have to strive to meet higher and higher standards to become more acceptable to God and to myself. I could be content to lose my life—to be nothing in and of myself—so that He could fill me with His life and could do His work through me. All that was required was to present myself to Him for His use.

When Jesus instructed His disciples to lose their lives for His sake, He was asking them to give up their *self*-striving, and *let Jesus live His life through them*. Paul said:

> I have been crucified with Christ [in Him I have shared His crucifixion]; it is no longer I who live, but Christ (the Messiah) lives in me. (Galatians 2:20)

> For me to live is Christ [His life in me]. (Philippians 1:21)

We are to be homes for Christ to live in on the earth. To lose our lives means to obey Him and to give up our self-glory, so that His glory may be shown.

Deny Yourself

Jesus says, "If anyone desires to be My disciple, let him deny himself [disregard, lose sight of, and forget himself and his own interests], and take up his cross and follow Me . . ." (Matthew 16:24). What does it mean to deny or forget ourselves?

Denying ourselves seems rather negative, unless we understand that we are to deny ourselves for a higher purpose. When we lay down our lives for Jesus to use, we really place our own worst enemy in His hands! Only He can make us whole so that we stop working against ourselves.

Forgetting ourselves begins with a deliberate choice. Clark, a successful bank executive, related, "I can remember a time when nothing was more important to me than a golf game with my boss on Saturdays. I enjoyed golf, and I thought the association would benefit my career. I did feel guilty about not spending more time with my wife and sons, but I told myself they would benefit materially from my choice. A few years ago, I felt that God was showing me I needed to spend more time with my family. The first couple of Saturdays that I stayed at home, my boss was displeased and really gave me a hard time. I wondered if I had done the right thing. But I decided to trust God with the outcome. And, you know what? I have never been happier—in my job and at home!"

Our minds cannot be surrendered to Jesus and to our own way at the same time. When He enables us to forget ourselves, we can be assured that He will see that our needs are met. When we "seek (aim at and strive after) first of all His kingdom and His righteousness (His way of doing and being right), . . . then all these things taken together will be given you besides" (Matthew 6:33).

"Take Up Your Cross"

The concept of taking up the cross may be frightening. One woman said, "I'm afraid of my cross! Will it be some terrible sickness or tragedy? When my husband left me, my mother told me that his leaving was my cross to bear!"

Others think that if they take up their cross, they must leave immediately for the mission field or do something that would be the one thing they hated the most.

Jane laughingly related, "When I heard the phrase 'to take up your cross,' I imagined myself standing over a hot stove, stirring a large pot of stew. I remember thinking, *I can see myself now! God is going to make me run a soup kitchen from my house! And I can't even cook! There will be people lined up at my front walk and filing through my house! I don't think I can bear it!*"

When we misunderstand what Jesus meant when He said that we were to take up our cross, we miss a rich experience. What does your friend believe about her cross? Is she still centered on herself and her own needs, or is she free to care about others? Is she afraid that her cross will be sickness? Abandonment? Loss of some kind? Teach her what God's Word says about the Cross.

Remember that our cross and the Cross of Jesus are not the same. On His Cross, Jesus bore our "griefs (sicknesses, weaknesses, and distresses) and carried our sorrows and pains [of punishment]. . . . He was wounded for our transgressions, He was bruised for our guilt and iniquities; the chastisement [needful to obtain], peace and well-being for us was upon Him . . ." (Isaiah 53:4–5). Since He has already borne these things for us and in our place, we don't have to bear these as our crosses.

Our cross consists of whatever difficulties arise as a result of our service to God. Taking up our cross with the willingness to face difficulty is a voluntary action. For example, our cross may be enduring the persecution of business associates when we stand for what is right on critical issues. Or our cross may be leaving one job to begin a ministry. Our cross may involve the pain of severing ungodly relationships so that we can follow Jesus without distractions or hindrances or doing without something we want so that we can meet the need of someone else. Our cross may involve letting go of our own pride in order to help someone else.

"Our cross consists of whatever difficulties arise as a result of our service to God. Taking up our cross with the willingness to face difficulty is a voluntary action."

Regardless of the difficulty or sacrifice required, when we take up our cross, the power of God will enable us to carry it. Our Father will be glorified, and we will grow closer to Him for having obeyed His instructions.

"And Follow Me"

Not long ago, I was driving home from a meeting late at night. It was foggy and rainy, and I was beginning to feel uneasy, when ahead of me, I saw the taillights of my neighbor's car. Throughout the drive home, as long as I could see her car, I didn't worry. I had a beacon to follow, and I knew I wouldn't get lost.

Following Jesus is not burdensome or heavy. In fact, Jesus said:

> Come to Me, all you who labor and are heavy-laden and overburdened, and I will cause you to rest. [I will ease and relieve and refresh your souls.] Take My yoke upon you and learn of Me, for I am gentle (meek) and humble (lowly) in heart, and you will find rest (relief and ease and refreshment and recreation and blessed quiet) for your souls. For My yoke is wholesome (useful, good—not harsh, hard, sharp, or pressing, but comfortable, gracious, and pleasant), and My burden is light and easy to be borne. (Matthew 11:28–30)

When we follow Jesus—when we lean on Him and not on ourselves—"He will direct and make straight and plain your paths" (Proverbs 3:5–6).

True self-esteem is not found within the *self*, but through a relationship with Jesus in which you love and serve Him. Does your friend have this kind of relationship with Jesus? Does she understand how to follow Him? Does she know how much He loves her?

Ways to Help

The answers to these questions will guide you in your counsel with your friend. Your friend needs to esteem Jesus in her life, not self. Give your friend a period of time to make choices. She may not be ready to let go of old patterns of behaving and thinking. Death to the self is painful!

Guide Her in Leaving the Path of Self

When she is ready, help your friend work through the following steps. You may need to spend more time on some steps and less on others, so ask the Spirit to help you be aware of her pace. Listen with your heart!

1. In prayer, repent of self-centeredness and pride.

2. Admit the need for God's love, as well as the love of others.

3. Ask forgiveness for ways you have harmed others. Humble yourself before God and others by making restitution if God directs.

4. Commit your life to God's plan. Give up your own way.

5. Study the life of Jesus, being open to being changed into His image.

6. Seek to make love your aim.

Help Her to Treat Herself Kindly

Remind your friend that she is to treat herself with the same love, compassion, and mercy the Father extends to her.

Your friend may expect more of herself than she does of other people. If so, she may criticize herself harshly when she makes a mistake or fails. Help her to assess her strengths and weaknesses realistically, reminding her that "it is God Who is all the while effectually at work" in her, creating in her "[the power and desire] both to will and to work for His good pleasure and satisfaction and delight" (Philippians 2:13). When she makes mistakes, encourage her to give herself the understanding and compassion that she would offer to a friend. Encourage her to speak kindly to herself, accept her limitations with humor, and be quick to forgive herself.

For example, one of my friends had a bad habit of berating herself every time she made a mistake playing tennis. Soon after discussing this, she missed an easy shot. She exclaimed, "I did it! Instead of calling myself 'stupid,' I was able to say, 'Now that's okay, sweet thing. You just try that again!' What a difference it made in my entire attitude!"

Encourage a Balanced Lifestyle

Denying ourselves and forgetting ourselves is not the same as neglecting to care for our minds, spirits, and bodies. We must realize the implications of these words: "your body is the temple (the very sanctuary) of the Holy Spirit Who lives within you" (1 Corinthians 6:19).

Help your friend take care of herself physically, mentally, and emotionally. Exercise, good nutrition, mental stimulation, rest, and recreation are all important ingredients in maintaining a healthy body and mind. Encourage her to relax by listening to music, reading, enjoying nature, or taking a relaxing bath. Find the little things she can do to care for and celebrate the person God has created her to be.

The Importance of Laughter

Laughter also has healing power. It not only heals the mind but also the body! Proverbs 15:15 says that "he who has a glad heart has a continual feast [regardless of circumstances]." Proverbs 17:22 further advises that "A happy heart is good medicine and a cheerful mind works healing."

Find things to laugh about. Try to see the humorous side of life. Look for things to be thankful and happy about.

Read funny books or watch humorous movies. Don't take everything so seriously. Remember that Jesus enjoyed people, weddings, feasts, parties, and laughter. Learn to laugh!

The Importance of Tears

Tears are just as important as laughter and can cleanse the soul. When your friend feels sad, encourage her to have a good cry. When we bottle up emotions, they are released when we least want them to be!

The Secret of Self-esteem

I watched the potter in amazement as he took the shapeless lump of wet clay and spun it on his wheel. Up and down the wheel turned, and with each turn, the formless clay took on shape. First, a cylinder, then a rounded lip emerged. Before my eyes, the shape of a vase was produced.

But then, a crack in the clay appeared. The man seemed undisturbed. Without breaking his rhythm, he molded it back into the pattern, creating again a thing of beauty.

The clay had no work to do, except to be molded by the potter's hand. A verse from Jeremiah came to mind, "Behold, as the clay is in the potter's hand, so are you in My hand" (Jeremiah 18:6). I thought of how hard I had worked to have a good self-esteem, to make myself acceptable to God, give Him cause to be proud of me—and how miserably I had failed. My strivings had been useless. How simple it was just to be the clay, molded and shaped by the loving hand of the Father!

The secret of self-esteem is found in a personal relationship with God. As we continue to know Him, to behold His glory, to walk with Him in surrender and obedience, we will be "transfigured into His very own image" (2 Corinthians 3:18). To be made into the image of Christ is our highest glory!

LIFE APPLICATIONS _____

1. What do you think of when someone says they have a low self-esteem? According to your definition, do you have a low or high self-esteem?

2. What is the difference between loving yourself and not thinking too highly of yourself? Can people be humble and love themselves?

3. Have you ever felt that you didn't know why God created you? Have you been without direction?

4. Do you know someone who continually strives for approval? In your opinion, what is her general emotional state?

5. If someone said to you, "Who are you?" how would you answer? Is your answer based on externals (what you do, to whom you are married, where you live, etc.)?

6. Why is knowing Jesus and having a right relationship with the Father the only true basis for a healthy self-esteem?

7. Do you agree that your "self" is your worst enemy? Would you like to "lose yourself"? Why?

8. What did Jesus mean when He said, "Take up your cross and follow Me"? Why is that God's answer to

the self-esteem problem? What have been your "crosses"?

9. Have you ever known anyone who passionately wanted to serve Christ and was serving Him effectively? Would you want to be like that person? Why?

14

ILLNESS

Heal me, O Lord, and I shall be healed; save me,
and I shall be saved; for You are my praise.

JEREMIAH 17:14

I've been sick so long that sometimes I wonder if I'll ever
be well," Carol told me. "It's so hard for me not to be
able to take care of my little boys and my husband. I feel
guilty for being so sick for so long. At times I think I'm just
imagining all my symptoms—that it's all in my head—
despite what my doctors say. It doesn't help when people
say, 'You *always* have something wrong with you!' or 'I've
never known anybody who was sick as much as you are!'
Their reactions bother me almost as much as the physical
pain. Maybe I should accept the fact that I'll always be sick
and that nobody will ever understand! Can you help me?"

Carol is one of many who have felt the physical and
emotional agony of an illness. Discouragement, guilt, anger, disappointment, frustration, pain, lack of control, feelings of usefulness, fear—these are the insidious partners of
disease that make illness so difficult to bear. How can you
help a friend who is sick? What can you say to give her
hope, encouragement, and relief?

The greatest need of those who are chronically ill is not for sympathy, nor is it the need for pat answers. Although they may appreciate your compassion and concern, they want relief from their pain. They need to know God's Word, which will provide truth and lead to healing.

You will not be able to effectively help or offer hope to a sick friend unless you are convinced that it is God's will for her to be well. You can only offer hope if you know that God has made provision for her healing in His Word.

Is Sickness God's Will?

This is a question you must allow God to settle in your mind once and for all. The quality of help you give to your friend depends on it! What do you believe is God's will for your friend? Do you believe He made her sick? Do you believe He wants her to suffer illness for some spiritual purpose? Do you believe He wants her to get well? Will He help her?

Because there are many various philosophies regarding healing today, it is important to carefully consider what God's Word says. By looking at the words of God our Father, the life and death of Jesus, and the work of the Holy Spirit, we can begin to understand God's will about healing.

God the Father—Our Doctor

In the book of Exodus, God first introduces Himself as our Healer. Speaking to Moses and the Israelites, He says, "If you will diligently hearken to the voice of the Lord your God and will do what is right in His sight, and will listen to and obey His commandments and keep all His statutes, I will put none of the diseases upon you which I brought upon the Egyptians, for *I am the Lord Who heals you*" (Exodus 15:26, emphasis added). The word used for "Lord" in this verse is *rapha*, the Hebrew word for "doctor." God the Father makes it clear that He is our Doctor who heals all our diseases (see also Psalm 103:3).

Some think that because medical science has progressed so far, God no longer functions in the role of Healer. However, Malachi 3:6 says, "For I am the Lord, I do not change."

One woman joyfully told me, "I'd tried everything. My doctors had given up on me, so I began to try to adjust to the fact I would never be well. Then an old friend moved back to town. She began telling me about God's desire to be my Healer. She began to visit me every week and to pray for me. I was pretty skeptical, but she seemed so sincere, and I figured I didn't have anything to lose! Several months later at my next check-up, you can imagine how astonished I was when tests showed a radical improvement in my condition. The doctors were surprised, too, and said they couldn't take any credit for my improvement. I have continued to pray with my friend and my symptoms are almost entirely gone! I thank God for sending me a friend who knew God as her Doctor!"

"You will not be able to effectively help or offer hope to a sick friend unless you are convinced that it is God's will for her to be well."

The Life and Death of Jesus

Each act and step in the *life* of Jesus was directed by God the Father. Jesus said, "For I have come down from heaven not to do My own will and purpose but to do the will and purpose of Him Who sent Me" (John 6:38). The Gospels record many of the healings of Jesus. He did not turn people away because their disease was too critical, or because they had been sick too long, or because they did not deserve to be well. He healed a leper (Matthew 8:2–3), two blind men (Matthew 9:27–31), a woman who had been sick for twelve years (Luke 8:43–48), as well as a man who had been sick for thirty-eight years (John 5:5–9). He forgave a paralyzed man his sins, and the man walked (Mark 2:3–12), and He healed many who did not even know Him (Matthew 8:5–13 and Mark 9:17–27). When Jesus healed the sick, He was following the direction of His Father, God the Healer.

The *death* of Jesus on the Cross was the Father's provision for our healing. Isaiah portrays a picture of Jesus giving us healing through His death on the Cross, saying, "Surely He has borne our griefs (sicknesses, weaknesses, and distresses) and carried our sorrows and pains [of punishment]" (Isaiah 53:4). Although many of us know that Jesus took our sins upon Himself on the Cross, many do not realize that He also took our sicknesses. In fact, the word *save* means to deliver, to protect, to preserve, *to heal*, and to make whole. Faith for healing can grow tremendously just from understanding that healing, as well as forgiveness of sins, was given through the shed blood of Jesus on the Cross.

A woman recovering from a heart condition told me, "I knew that when Jesus saved me, He gave me eternal life, but I didn't realize He gave me healing, too. I had the idea that God might want me to be sick for some reason. But He doesn't want me to be sick any more than He wanted me to be lost! Since I realized the entire truth about my salvation, I am developing the same confidence about getting well as I have about going to heaven!"

The Work of the Holy Spirit

When Jesus went to heaven, He sent the Holy Spirit back to live in us and to work among us. The Holy Spirit is the One who comforts us, teaches us (John 14:26), and intercedes for us (Romans 8:27). In addition, one of the gifts of the Holy Spirit is the gift of healing (1 Corinthians 12:9). When we pray, it is the Holy Spirit Who actually carries out the will of the Father and the Son by performing the healing in us.

Help your friend to understand that all three Persons in the Godhead desire her healing. God the Father is her Doctor, Jesus made her healing possible today through His death on the Cross, and the Holy Spirit performs the work in her. It is not the will of the Father, the Son, or the Holy Spirit for her to be sick! It is God's will for His children to enjoy health, in all aspects of life!

"The death of Jesus on the Cross was the Father's provision for our healing."

Hindrances to Healing

Although it is God's will for His children to be healthy, there are some hindrances to receiving total healing, whether it be healing of the mind, body, or the spirit. As you comfort a friend who is sick, listen carefully to her conversation. Pray for discernment to recognize guilt, false guilt, bitterness, anger, fear, worry, and chronic grief or regret. These emotions can drastically affect recovery from illness. Listen for phrases like "When I think about him, my stomach gets in a knot," or "She is just a pain in the neck," or "That just makes me sick!" or "I'm just too sick to . . . ," or "I'll never get over that as long as I live!" Our bodies can actually hear these expressions as instructions and respond accordingly!

Lack of Knowledge

Hosea 4:6 says, "My people are destroyed for lack of knowledge." Does your friend know that God's will is her wholeness, and that He has made a way for her to receive His healing?

Lack of Trust

"Why is my pain perpetual and my wound incurable, refusing to be healed? Will You indeed be to me like a deceitful brook, like waters that fail and are uncertain?" (Jeremiah 15:18). If your friend has believed that it is God's will for her to remain sick, it will take time for her to be free of the same doubt that Jeremiah experienced.

Many people who have been ill for an extended time begin to question God's desire to heal, and so they find it difficult to continue to entrust themselves to His care. God's gentle but firm response to Jeremiah was this:

> If you return [and give up this mistaken tone of distrust and despair], then I will give you again a settled place of quiet and safety, and you will be My minister; and if you separate the precious from the vile [cleansing your own heart from unworthy and unwarranted suspicions con-

cerning God's faithfulness], you shall be as My mouth-piece. (Jeremiah 15:19)

Need for Attention

Do you know people who are so conditioned to receiving attention because of their illness that it is difficult for them to recover? One woman told her pastor, "People are always so kind to ask about my health. They visit me because I'm a shut-in. How do I know anyone would come to see me if I got well?" For this woman, the thought of giving up her illness was frightening; it had become her protection against loneliness.

Fear of Recovery

Some who are ill have become accustomed to a limited life-style, and they may even feel they have lost the skills necessary for daily tasks. They may choose to remain in the relative safety of illness rather than to venture out into the world as responsible people. One woman who had been confined to a wheelchair for many months confided to me her fears of recovery. She said, "It's been so long since I drove or did anything without this wheelchair, I'm afraid I won't know how! I know this is crazy, but sometimes I find myself not really wanting to get well!"

Desire to Control

Illness can be used to influence the behavior of others. For example, a mother who cannot control her teenager's behavior may succumb to headaches when her child begins to overwhelm her. Suddenly the house must become quiet, and conflict must cease. It is tempting to want to use sickness to retain some sense of power!

Holding On to a Bad Habit

Some people are unwilling to change harmful habits to regain health. A seriously overweight woman told me, "My doctor told me to lose weight and get my cholesterol level down, but it's just not happening!" When asked about her diet, she replied, "I've eaten fried foods all my life! They're my favorite! I can't give them up. There's just got to be another way!"

The Need for Punishment

Your friend may believe she deserves to be sick because of past sins in her life. In spite of repentance and a changed lifestyle, she may feel (consciously or unconsciously) that she must continue to pay a price for her sin—illness! She does not understand God's grace.

With tears in her eyes and pain etched on her face, one woman confessed, "A few months ago, I committed adultery. I just learned that I contracted the herpes virus. I can't believe God would heal me of this condition. I got it because I broke one of the Ten Commandments!"

Unconfessed Sin

Healing involves the total person. God is concerned about relieving a person's physical symptoms, but He is more interested in healing the whole person—mind, body, and spirit! Sometimes "disease" is not the root problem. In order for anyone to become symptom-free, healing of our deeper problems must occur.

In *The Meaning of Persons* (Harper and Row: New York, 1957, p. 157), Dr. Paul Tournier wrote:

> A bad conscience can, over a period of years, so strangle a person's life that his physical and psychical powers of resistance are thereby impaired. It can be the root cause of

certain psychosomatic afflictions. It is like a stopper which can be pulled out by confession, so that life begins at once to flow again. That is why Dr. Sonderegger called the doctor the "natural confessor of humanity"; and why Michelet wrote that "a complete confession is always necessary in medicine."

The apostle James wrote: "Confess to one another therefore your faults (your slips, your false steps, your offenses, your sins) and pray [also] for one another, that you may be healed and restored [to a spiritual tone of mind and heart]" (James 5:16).

Lack of Obedience

A guilty conscience results from disobedience in some area of life. It is difficult to trust God for healing when we avoid Him because we have not done or are unwilling to do what He has asked.

The Gospel of John tells the story of an unusual instruction Jesus gave a man who had been blind from birth. After Jesus had spat on the ground and made mud, He applied the mixture to the man's eyes, and instructed him saying, "Go, wash in the Pool of Siloam" (John 9:7). When the man went to wash in the pool, he returned able to see (John 9:7). Obedience to this unusual instruction was the key to receiving sight!

Instructions to a sick person may involve letting go of past resentments, making restitution, or humbling herself in a relationship. Unforgiveness, bitterness, resentment, and unresolved relationships can block healing. When God gives a direction to someone who is ill, it is important for her to obey, even if she doesn't understand or the direction is difficult.

If you believe that your friend's healing may be delayed

due to her attitudes, ask God to give you wisdom. You may need to spend some time in prayer for your friend, or you may need to address the problem in a kind, tactful way. For example, you might ask, "Do you think that your anger might be draining your energy?" or "Does worry make you feel tense? Would you feel better if you were more relaxed?" When you feel that you need to confront a problem, it is important to assure your friend that you are looking at ways to contribute to her well-being. Avoid being critical, but give her opportunity to consider her answers to your questions and begin to think along with you.

A word of caution: If your friend is not recovering, don't assume that it must be because of a bad attitude or a lack of faith. Even though it is God's will for His children to be well, some do not recover, and some die. It is impossible to know all the reasons *why* this happens, because we cannot know everything about each person and her life. We must accept the fact that there are things we will never know this side of heaven.

If your friend is not recovering, it can become tempting to blame her or to blame yourself. *Don't blame anyone.* Simply continue to offer your love and prayers, trust Him with the outcome, and look for ways her overall life is changing for the good.

Ways to Help

Healing—in whatever form—comes from the Lord. You can help your friend through the process of seeking Him for the answers.

Use God's Word

The Word of God is alive, powerful, energizing, and active (Hebrews 4:12). When It enters our minds, It actually transforms our thinking. The psalmist saw it this way: "He sends forth His word and heals them and rescues them from the pit and destruction" (Psalm 107:20). God's Word heals!

Use the Scriptures to teach your friend that God wants her to be well in mind, body, and spirit. Encourage her to read the Gospels and the book of Acts. Together, study the Bible's teaching concerning healing. Provide Scripture tapes and testimonies; encourage her to listen to them often. Follow the advice of Proverbs: "My son, attend to my words; consent and submit to my sayings. Let them not depart from your sight; keep them in the center of your heart. For they are life to those who find them, healing and health to all their flesh" (Proverbs 4:20–22).

Carol recalled how using the Word had given her peace when she was afraid to be put to sleep before surgery. "I had memorized Psalm 121, and while the nurses were getting me ready for surgery, God reminded me that He would not slumber nor sleep while I was in surgery and that He would keep me from harm. While the anesthesiologist was putting in my IV, I was able to thank Him and I found myself silently singing the hymn 'It Is Well with My Soul' until I went to sleep."

Prayer

James 5:16 says, "The earnest heartfelt, continued prayer of a righteous man makes tremendous power available [dynamic in its working]." Prayer draws us closer to our Father, as well as to one another. Don't be afraid to pray with your friend. Use the words that are on your heart for her. A prayer from the heart is dynamic!

You don't have to have the "right" words or pray according to a specific formula for God to hear you. The Bible records many ways of praying for the sick.

Laying on of Hands. Many times when Jesus prayed for the sick, He reached out and touched them (Mark 6:5; 7:32–35; 16:18; Luke 4:40; 13:13). As He laid His hands on them, they became well. His touch transmitted the healing power of His Father to their minds, spirits, and bodies. It transmitted His compassion for their suffering. His touch healed.

"Healing—in whatever form—comes from the Lord."

The Name of Jesus. As Jesus prepared to return to His Father, He instructed His disciples to preach the Gospel everywhere, saying that all who believed in Him would lay hands on the sick *in His name* and they would recover (Mark 16:16–18). Because the name of Jesus is above every name (Ephesians 1:18–23; Philippians 2:9–10), the touch of a friend, praying in the name of Jesus, is powerful.

Anointing with Oil. Another way the Bible teaches us to intercede for a sick friend is by calling the leadership of the church to pray for the person, anointing her with oil. The apostle James told how it was to be done:

> Is anyone among you sick? He should call in the church elders (the spiritual guides) and they should pray over him, anointing him with oil in the Lord's name. And the prayer [that is] of faith will save him who is sick, and the Lord will restore him; and if he has committed sins, he will be forgiven. (James 5:14-15)

Throughout the Bible, oil often is used as a symbol of the Holy Spirit. Anointing your friend with oil is a graphic

236

representation of the work of the Holy Spirit's ministry of healing.

The Prayer of Faith. You may be thinking you don't have enough faith to pray for someone who is sick. It is sometimes overwhelming to imagine how much faith it must take to pray for a miracle! But Jesus told us if we have faith as small as a mustard seed, we can move mountains (Matthew 17:20). It has been said, "We can have a little faith in a big God." If you feel you are lacking in faith, ask the Father to give you the faith to pray for your friend. Spend time in the Word. Faith comes from getting to know God and hearing the Word of Christ (Romans 10:17).

Faith is important because it is *a defensive weapon against Satan and his works.* John 10:10 tells us that Jesus came to give us abundant life, while Satan's intentions are to steal, kill, and destroy. There are many instances in the Bible where Jesus healed those whose sickness was attributed to Satan. The Gospel of Luke tells of a woman who "for eighteen years had had an infirmity caused by a spirit (a demon of sickness). She was bent completely forward and utterly unable to straighten herself up or to look forward" (Luke 13:11). When Jesus laid His hands on her, she was instantly cured!

Ask your Father to show you how to pray for your friend. If you feel your faith is weak, ask Him to give you the gift of faith for your friend. Never underestimate the power of prayer. It is the avenue by which God allows you to be a part of the demonstration of His power!

Encourage Your Friend to Help Others

Helping, serving, and comforting another, even in small ways, will dispel any notion that she is useless and will give your friend a sense of purpose. Not only will she be reminded of her usefulness to God, but she will also remain connected with the outside world.

Encourage her not to "wait until . . ." to serve Him. Teach her how to redeem her time loving God and others. For example, bring her greeting cards to mail to others or encourage her to call someone who needs a cheerful word.

Help Your Friend Get Information

Knowledge about your friend's condition and medications can relieve the anxiety—both yours and hers—that is fed by ignorance. Gerald observed, "I couldn't understand why I was so tired all the time. My wife thought I was neglecting her. Neither of us knew that the medicine I was taking was making me lethargic. I was relieved when I learned what was wrong."

God has given us much knowledge through medical science and technology. Help your friend to take advantage of the resources that God has made available.

Plan Diversions

It is important that your relationship with your friend not revolve around her illness. She is a *person*, not an illness. She herself may tend to forget that, if she has been sick for a long time, so it is important to spend some time doing things together that do not relate to illness. If she is able, plan a drive on a sunny day or find interesting articles to share. A simple thing like getting an ice cream cone may be extremely refreshing to someone who has been shut in.

If your friend's room is dark, ask if you may open the curtains and let the sunshine in. God's creation speaks cheerful thoughts! Move her bed near a window. Give her music tapes to play. Beautiful music will lift her spirits.

A Merry Heart

A merry heart does good like a medicine (Proverbs 17:22). Pass along funny stories and humorous observations to your friend. Help her to recall humorous events in her life. Share yours with her. Rent funny movies. Laughter is healing.

Ask Your Friend to Pray for You

Since you are a helper, you may appear to be coming from a position of greater strength. Your friend may assume that your life is in total order and that all your needs are met. Let your friend know that you also need *her* prayers and that she can add something to your life.

Avoid Reinforcing Self-pity

We tend to indulge ourselves in self-pity when we feel hopeless. If your friend has been sick for a long while or is in constant pain, it is easy to succumb to a feeling of hopelessness. Avoid reinforcing your friend's self-pity, but instead offer hope.

Hope is more than simply encouraging your friend or telling her she will feel better. Hope is more than positive thinking. Hope is believing that God, the Creator of the universe "cares for you affectionately and cares about you watchfully" (1 Peter 5:7). Hope is knowing that God "gives power to the faint and weary, and to him who has no might. He increases strength" (Isaiah 40:29). Share with your friend the hope that you have experienced with your Father. Help her to hope in God, not in her healing or how her body feels.

Continually Give Thanks

Encourage your friend to continually give thanks to God for her blessings. This will help her to focus on what she does have, rather than on what she doesn't have. Hebrews 13:15 tells us "Through Him, therefore, let us constantly and at all times offer up to God a sacrifice of praise, which is the fruit of lips that thankfully acknowledge and confess and glorify His name."

Show Respect for the Beliefs of Your Friend

Some may never believe that God will heal them. They may refer to the fact that God never healed Paul of his "thorn in the flesh" (2 Corinthians 12:7–9). Although we do not know specifically what this thorn was, Paul describes it as "a messenger of Satan, to wrack and buffet and harass me, to keep me from becoming excessively exalted" (2 Corinthians 12:7). God told Paul that He would not remove this thorn, but He would strengthen him in his weakness.

If your friend sincerely believes that God has spoken the same words to her, accept her explanation and be of comfort to her in any way that you can. We cannot know what God speaks to the heart of another. We do not know or understand all of God's mysteries. Pray that if your friend is mistaken, God will reveal her error to her, and, whether she is healed or not, that God will be glorified in her life!

True Healing

I believe that it is God's will for His children to be well and whole in mind, body, and spirit. This recovery may be an extended process, using many avenues of healing, or it may be an instantaneous work of the Spirit.

We must always remember, however, that *our highest purpose is not to be healed but to know and to love God.* Our highest calling is to reflect the love of Jesus to others. As you work with those who are sick, point them to the

Father Who heals, the Son Who saves, and the Spirit Who performs the will of the Father and Son. Give them the hope of Malachi 4:2:

> But unto you who revere and worshipfully fear My name shall the Sun of Righteousness arise with healing in His wings and His beams, and you shall go forth and gambol like calves [released] from the stall and leap for joy.

LIFE APPLICATIONS

1. Have you ever suffered from a long-term illness? Did anyone help you during that time? How?

2. Do you believe that God's highest desire is for you to be well?

3. How many advances in the field of medicine can you think of that have been made in the last twenty years? Do you see these advances as God's provisions for healing?

4. Have you known anyone who appeared to enjoy their illness? How did you feel toward them?

5. Have you ever felt that you deserved to be sick? Why? What would you tell someone who believed that today?

6. Have you ever felt ashamed when you remained sick after people prayed for you? Do you see healing as a process?

7. Do you know of someone who is sick or badly handi-

capped who is a strong witness for Jesus? What strengths do they have?

8. Have you ever known anyone who experienced a healing miracle?

9. Read aloud James 5:13–16.

15

TEMPTATION

For because He Himself [in His humanity] has suffered in
being tempted (tested and tried), He is able [immediately]
to run to the cry of (assist, relieve) those who are being
tempted and tested and tried [and who therefore
are being exposed to suffering].

HEBREWS 2:18

I knew it was wrong to be dishonest on my income tax.
But, I really needed that money, and I figured, who
would ever know?"

"I never cheated on my wife before! I don't know what
happened! Suddenly, I was in another woman's arms!"

Temptations are everywhere. How can you help a
friend resist the allure of a temptation? How can *you* resist
temptations?

Catherine was in her early forties when her husband
announced he was leaving her to live with another woman.
The following year was a lonely period of adjustment for
her. As her first Christmas without her husband neared, the
wife of an old friend died. Soon the widowed husband,
Ray, began to invite Catherine to dinner. Grateful for companionship, she began to spend every Friday night with

him. Ray lived in another city, so rather than insist that he spend money on a motel, she offered him her spare bedroom.

Catherine was lonely, so she continued to see Ray, even though she was aware that God's Word cautioned against Christians dating non-Christians (2 Corinthians 6:14). He had firmly informed her that he was not interested in religious matters, although he did not object to *her* faith. Having become emotionally involved with Ray, she told herself, "Maybe God brought Ray to me so that I could witness to him. Maybe God knew I could witness in ways that his wife couldn't. I'll just continue to pray, and I know everything will work out somehow. God has always been so faithful in the past. He won't let me down now."

Six months passed, during which Catherine's feelings for Ray deepened. Having spent every weekend together, they had become emotionally dependent upon each other, as well as sexually intimate. Although Catherine attended church, and Ray occasionally went also, he seemed no nearer to salvation than he had been when they first met.

"I don't know what I'm going to do," cried Catherine. "I feel far from God, and I'm ashamed of my choice. My daughters realize Ray spends weekends with me, and I sense their disbelief and disappointment. In fact, they won't even come home anymore!"

"I've tried to break up with Ray, but my decision doesn't stand very long. Every time I give in, I feel worse. I don't think Ray will ever marry me, and why should he? I've given him all I have already! Now I'm so confused that I don't know if I really want to marry him anymore!"

Temptation is constant and no one is immune. We must not underestimate its power to draw and deceive. Not even Jesus was protected from it.

The Temptations of Jesus

The temptations experienced by Jesus in the wilderness are temptations common to all of us. The apostle John summarized them:

> For all that is in the world—the lust of the flesh [craving for sensual gratification] and the lust of the eyes [greedy longings of the mind] and the pride of life [assurance in one's own resources or in the stability of earthly things]— these do not come from the Father but are from the world [itself]. (1 John 2:16)

Jesus was tempted in every way that we are tempted, yet He successfully resisted (Hebrews 4:15). You will find that as you help others, their struggles with temptation fall into these three categories: the lust of the flesh, the lust of the eyes, or the pride of life.

"Temptation is constant and no one is immune. . . . Not even Jesus was protected from it."

The Lust of the Flesh

Lusts of the flesh involve any temptation that appeals to our physical senses. Lust is a natural desire that has deviated from God's purpose and has become harmful. Temptation always originates from a real need or want. Jesus' first temptation arose from a need for food. He had no food for forty days and was hungry when Satan said to Him, "If You are God's Son, command these stones to be made [loaves of] bread" (Matthew 4:3). Jesus replied, "Man shall not live and be upheld and sustained by bread alone, but by every word that comes forth from the mouth of God" (Matthew 4:4).

Satan attempted to persuade Jesus to have His need for food met in the wrong way, but Jesus resisted Satan by His knowledge of Scripture (Matthew 4:4). Then, after Jesus overcame Satan, God filled His need by sending angels to feed and minister to Him (Matthew 4:11).

Chris, a woman in her early thirties, related, "I can't explain the emotional attachment I began to feel for my pastor after I started to see him for counseling. I was abused by my father, and no man had ever been gentle or sympathetic to me before. His kindness really touched my heart.

"One day, as I left his office, he put his arms around me and kissed me on the cheek. I was horrified to discover I desired him physically. At that point, I knew I should stop going to his office, but I didn't. I told myself he would never know my feelings, but then he explained that he was also attracted to me! I felt terrible, because we had even prayed together that God would send me a kind man to love! I realized that I had become so emotionally entrapped that only my pastor's love would satisfy me! I felt that I had to have him!"

Satan took advantage of Chris's need for kindness and human touch from a man. But she was defeated when she chose something immediate and forbidden rather than to wait in faith for God to answer her prayer.

The Lust of the Eye

Lusts of the eye include material possessions, position, relationships, or recognition—anything that will make us look good to others. Satan tempted Jesus to bring glory and attention to Himself by performing a spectacular feat.

Satan took Jesus to a mountaintop and tempted him saying, "If you are the Son of God, throw Yourself down; for it is written, He will give His angels charge over you, and they will bear you up on their hands, lest you strike your foot against a stone" (Matthew 4:6). When Satan tried to convince Jesus that God would keep Him safe, regardless of His motives or actions, Jesus was once again able to defeat him by knowledge of and obedience to His Father's Word (Matthew 4:7).

Tom traveled from city to city preaching evangelistic crusades. One night, leaving late for his destination, he drove far above the speed limit, praying, "Lord, don't let me get caught!" As he sped down the highway, he was frantic when he heard the siren of a police car. "Oh, Lord," he prayed, "please don't let him give me a ticket!"

We can become tempted when we expect God to follow and protect *us* wherever *we* desire to go, to meet all of our "wants" as well as our needs, and to do it in *our* timing.

The Pride of Life

This temptation causes us to rely on our own resources and schemes instead of waiting on God. It says, "You can have it all! You have the power! Take charge of your life!" The pride of life tempts us to take our lives into our own hands—to be like God without depending on Him or being faithful to Him.

Satan showed Jesus all the kingdoms of the world and promised he would give it all to Him, if He would bow before him and worship him. Once again, Jesus defeated Satan with Scripture, saying, "Begone, Satan! For it has been written, You shall worship the Lord your God, and Him alone shall you serve" (Matthew 4:10).

James shook his head as he told the story of losing a job promotion. "An opening for promotion came in my company, and I really wanted it. I had worked hard and thought I had the company's interest at heart. When I learned I had a competitor for the promotion, I decided to tell our boss about some unethical actions he had taken in the past. To my surprise, my boss became angry and ordered me out of his office! He then hired my competitor, in spite of the information I had passed along! I thought my boss would appreciate my attempt to protect our company, but he didn't. By taking things into my own hands, I killed my chance for that promotion!"

Jesus was able to resist all temptations during His earthly ministry because He did only what His Father instructed Him to do (John 14:31). Jesus gave His Father full control over His life, remaining fully committed to His Father's *purposes and ways* of accomplishing them.

As you encourage others to resist temptations of the lust of the flesh, the lust of the eye, and the pride of life, point them to the example of Jesus. Also, be aware that temptations have stages.

The Progression of a Temptation

Temptation never comes from God. Temptation always originates from Satan or in our own minds. The apostle James says, "Let no one say when he is tempted, I am tempted from God; for God is incapable of being tempted by [what is] evil and He Himself tempts no one" (James 1:13).

James then explains temptation. He says:

But every person is tempted when he is drawn away, enticed and baited by his own evil desire (lust, passions).

Then the evil desire, when it has conceived, gives birth to
sin, and sin, when it is fully matured, brings forth death.
(James 1:14–15)

An Evil Desire

Temptation starts with an evil desire that we are tempted
to satisfy. These desires usually hit us when we are vulnerable. Jesus had gone without food for forty days and
nights. He was hungry! Satan used this vulnerability to
tempt Him.

Many times we are tempted with evil desires *after taking a spiritual step or after a spiritual victory*. Just prior to
being tempted, Jesus had been baptized and the Spirit of
God had descended upon Him (Matthew 3:16).

Temptation also works on our doubts. Satan tempted
Jesus with questions, such as, "Will God provide? Will God
protect? Will God do what He said He would do?" These
doubts tempt us to satisfy our own desires, instead of waiting upon God.

Entertaining the Evil Desire

Experiencing an evil desire does *not* mean that we have suc-
cumbed to temptation. It is what we *do* with the wrong
desire that determines whether or not we fall prey to sin.
All of us will be tempted. But when we entertain the evil
desire—play around with it in our heads—the evil desire is
"conceived" and "gives birth to sin" (James 1:15).

Taking Action

Eventually, entertaining the desire will cause us to take
action and to sin. After having thought about the desire, it
becomes easier and easier to put the thought into action.
And once the initial step is taken, it becomes more and
more difficult to stop.

Catherine was *vulnerable* to Ray's attentions after her own husband left her. She had also become very active in a local church and had begun taking many *spiritual steps*. However, when Ray came along, she began to *doubt* that God would send her a Christian husband. She *deceived* herself into thinking that she could help him.

"Experiencing an evil desire does not mean that we have succumbed to temptation."

After she began to date Ray, she fantasized, "I wonder what it would be like to be married to him, to be a couple again, to be more important than anyone else is to him? After all, my ex-husband treated me so badly—surely I deserve something! He may not be a Christian, but he's a good man."

As Catherine continued her fantasies, she imagined a beautiful engagement ring, her wedding day, and a new house—all with Ray. Such *enticing thoughts* fed her desires to be loved and cherished, and suddenly she found herself unable to be away from Ray for long. At this point, she *gave in* to his increasing pressure and her own desires and began to be involved with him sexually. For the first time, she began to feel anxious and depressed much of the time. Her initial elation faded.

As Catherine's anxiety increased, she exclaimed, "Ray is an obsession for me! Our relationship is causing me more grief than happiness. I break up with him, then I call him and apologize for breaking up! He doesn't believe anything

I say anymore—and neither do I! I've stopped going to church. I rarely pray or read my Bible. I just don't feel God will hear me as long as I'm seeing Ray. I've lost my self-respect, the respect of my children, and I don't think Ray really respects me either! In fact, I think he may be dating another woman during the week, but I'm afraid to ask. What am I going to do? I feel trapped!"

Sin never brings fulfillment. On the contrary, it brings depression, anxiety, guilt, obsession, separation from the Father, indecision, and a loss of joy and peace. Catherine had been open to an evil desire, had begun entertaining the evil desire, and had then made the choices that resulted in the effects of sin. She *was* a woman trapped!

Hindrances to Resisting Temptations

As you help others who have difficulty resisting temptation, be aware of common hindrances to resisting temptation.

Double-Mindedness

The Bible describes the double-minded person as one who is like "the billowing surge out at sea that is blown hither and thither and tossed by the wind . . . [For being as he is] a man of two minds (hesitating, dubious, irresolute), [he is] unstable and unreliable and uncertain about everything [he thinks, feels, decides]" (James 1:6, 8).

When we allow temptation to work its course, our minds become darkened as we are drawn closer to sin. Temptation is a powerful force that weakens the will and causes ambivalence. Satan's lies then only confuse us. When we entertain tempting thoughts, our desire for immediate, selfish gratification will intensify until we allow our desire to be satisfied in Satan's way.

Common Misconceptions

This is the only way I can get this need met. Catherine was grateful for Ray's interest and began to doubt that God would or could provide a husband for her. Afraid that Ray might be the only man interested in her, she was easy prey for this misconception. Doubt and impatience leave us open to believing that the *wrong* way is the *only* way the need will be met.

It couldn't be really wrong. After all, I know other Christians who do it. Mary was a new Christian who had had an alcohol and drug problem. Before becoming a Christian, most of her friends spent their free evenings bar-hopping, drinking, or smoking marijuana. When she joined a singles group at her church, she was surprised and a bit confused when several of the women asked her to go to a local nightclub for drinks after work one Friday. Had Mary not been determined to leave her old life behind, she could easily have yielded to these old temptations from her "Christian" friends.

No one will ever know. What will it hurt? No one will ever know? Psalm 10:11 notes that a person "thinks in his heart, God has quite forgotten; He has hidden His face; He will never see [my deed]." God watches over us, and He knows when we sin. If we continue to sin, we cannot count on God's protection.

Psalm 91 is often called the "Psalm of Protection." Verse 1 begins, "He who dwells in the secret place of the Most High shall remain stable and fixed under the shadow of the Almighty [Whose power no foe can withstand]." God's protection is conditional upon our obedience, and we cannot presume upon it regardless of actions. Only as we stay close to Him and live according to His will can we depend upon Him to protect us. It is dangerous to continue deliberately to act outside of God's will.

God will forgive me anyway. If we turn to God in repentance, He promises forgiveness (1 John 1:9). He knows our hearts, and He allows a period of grace during which He will warn and convict us of sin. However, we must not presume upon His grace.

Note Paul's warning: "Or are you [so blind as to] trifle with and presume upon and despise and underestimate the wealth of His kindness and forbearance and longsuffering patience? Are you unmindful or actually ignorant [of the fact] that God's kindness is intended to lead you to repent (to change your mind and inner man to accept God's will)?" (Romans 2:4).

If, after we receive His warnings, we continue to sin, we shall suffer the consequences of our actions.

But I deserve to have this! Those who have been hurt in life may come to believe that they deserve "special favors." Have you ever heard of a person described as having a chip on her shoulder? Life may deal us a hard blow, but it is unwise to attempt to make up for what is lacking by committing sin.

Jackie said, "I know that I shouldn't overeat the way I do. My doctor has told me that my weight is endangering my health, and my family worries about me constantly. But I have such a stressful job! I come home just worn out, and a bowl of ice cream just makes me *feel* better! Is that too much to ask?"

This type of rationale is often the starting point for various addictions. God does not want us to take Satan's ways to find relief from the strains of life. Jesus has offered peace that passes understanding (John 14:27, Philippians 4:7). We can receive His gifts without being endangered or committing sin.

It's okay to do this one thing. After all, I don't do that. We can find so many ways to rationalize what we do. In order to justify going our own way, we try to establish self-righteousness in some areas so that we can make allowances for ourselves in others.

One woman told me, "I know I shouldn't continue to scream at my children as I do. I really feel bad about it, but *at least* I work hard to provide a home for them! That's more than their good-for-nothing daddy does!"

We continue on in defeat when we try to "get credit" in one area so that we can condone sin in another. This kind of rationalizing keeps us from turning to God for strength, which He promises He will give for every need (Philippians 4:13, 19).

A Hardened Heart

Deliberate rebellion toward God over a period of time develops a hard heart. Paul warns believers, "Therefore, as the Holy Spirit says; Today, if you will hear His voice, do not harden your hearts, as [happened] in the rebellion [of Israel] and their provocation and embitterment [of Me] in the day of testing in the wilderness, where your fathers tried [My patience] and tested [My forbearance] . . ." (Hebrews 3:7–9).

If your friend has delayed facing a temptation or sin, it will become easier and easier for her to justify wrong choices. We can get to the point where we not only lie to others, but also we can begin to believe our own lies. We no longer recognize the truth (Romans 1:25).

As Catherine's affair with Ray continued, she said, "As

long as we are faithful to each other, it's really *as if* we're married. At least he's begun to attend church with me once in a while. Since I've not been able to break up with him, maybe God just wants me to have someone who loves me. I can't believe God wants me to be alone again!"

A Lack of Knowledge

Connie related, "I became a Christian soon after my divorce. I knew that it was wrong to have sexual relations with a married man, but I didn't know it was wrong to do with a single man. One day I heard a sermon about fornication. I had never heard of the word! When I asked a friend what it meant, she informed me that it referred to sex outside of marriage. I was shocked! I could see why God wouldn't want me to break up a marriage, but I couldn't see why He would care otherwise."

As you work with a friend who is tempted, don't take for granted that she has knowledge of God's Word concerning areas of morality. In today's society, many are confused, and others have decided to disregard His Word on the subject of sex.

What If Your Friend Does Not Tell You That She Is Being Tempted?

If your friend is being tempted, she may not choose to confide in anyone, because she may be ambivalent. If God leads you to warn your friend, consider His leading very seriously.

You may wonder, "How can I initiate a subject like that without sounding 'holier than thou'?"

Charlotte, a secretary in a large office, told me she noticed a friend in her office had become very intimate with a sales representative who visited their company. Because

Charlotte and her friend attended the same church, Charlotte wanted to warn her; but she was reluctant, fearing that she would seem accusing. Not knowing how to initiate her concern, she remained quiet.

If you suspect your friend is struggling with a temptation or has become a party to sin, before you approach her, make sure that your motive is that of a sincere, humble desire to help. Ask God to search your heart and reveal any trace of self-righteousness that might be within you, and pray to be filled with God's wisdom and love. If you approach your friend, be willing to help her through her time of deliverance, if she is willing for you to do so.

When you are satisfied that your motive is right, you might say, "I know how much God loves you, and I want you to know that I care about you, too. There have been times when I've had to struggle with temptations, and I've needed a friend. Please forgive me if I am mistaken, but I think that you may. . . ."

"As you work with a friend who is tempted, don't take for granted that she has knowledge of God's Word concerning areas of morality."

If your friend shares her struggle with you, assure her that you will be there to help. This is a good time to express the faith that you have in her. For example, you might say, "I have seen you walk closely with God for a long time, and I believe that you really want to do what is right."

If she will not be open with you and you still believe that she is being tempted, continue to pray, but do not approach her again unless God specifically leads you to do so. There will be times when you will simply have to watch a friend walk away from God, and this will cause you sorrow.

Jesus had to watch the rich, young ruler walk away from the requirements for salvation. Jesus did not run after him, nor did He try to make the requirements more appealing. The rich, young ruler left, however, with God's Word in His heart (Luke 18:18–25). If your friend rejects the truth you offer in love, remember that God's Word will perform the work which He designed it to do (Isaiah 55:11).

Ways to Help

In helping your friend face temptation, there are several ways you can counsel her.

Share the Father's Love

Throughout the Old Testament, God sent prophets to warn His people about the dangers of sin. As God spoke through Jeremiah, we can hear the intensity of His deep love and desire for us to walk with Him and know His love, as He says, "O sinful children, come home, for I am your Master and I will bring you again to the land of Israel—one from here and two from there, wherever you are scattered. And I will give you leaders after my own heart, who will guide you with wisdom and understanding" (Jeremiah 3:14–15, TLB).

God wants to be a companion to us. He says, "And I thought how wonderful it would be for you to be here among my children. I planned to give you part of this beautiful land, the finest in the world. I looked forward to your

257

calling me 'Father,' and thought that you would never turn away from me again" (Jeremiah 3:19, TLB).

Remind Her That God Provides Escape Routes

Assure your friend that God knows the afflictions that come upon us when we give in to temptation and that even when she is in the middle of a temptation, He will rescue her.

Frank was a young executive who had overcome cocaine addiction in his college years. He had secured a responsible position in a corporation where his peers used cocaine daily. Knowing his vulnerability in that area, as well as his need to feel compatible with his associates, he turned to God for help. For several months, he declined invitations to join his associates for the social hour following work. He asked several men at his church to pray with him, asking God to work on his behalf.

Upon his six-month evaluation, he was given an unexpected promotion and was moved to another office. Realizing soon that the use of cocaine was not a problem in his new department, he was able to thank God for delivering him from temptation.

God provides for us even in the midst of temptation. Paul said:

> [No temptation or trial has come to you that is beyond human resistance and that is not adjusted and adapted and belonging to human experience, and such as man can bear.] But God is faithful [to His Word and to His compassionate nature], and He [can be trusted] not to let you be tempted and tried and assayed beyond your ability and strength of resistance and power to endure, but with the temptation, He will [always] also provide the way out (the means of escape to a landing place), that you may be

capable and strong and powerful to bear up under it patiently. (1 Corinthians 10:13)

Recognize Vulnerable Areas

Help your friend to recognize the situations or cues that create temptation. What reminds her or turns her thoughts toward the sin? Are there friends who draw her away from God? Are certain places associated with the temptation? Certain music? Knowledge of her personal vulnerable areas will help her to avoid situations that weaken her will.

Mary told me of the effort it took to break a habit of gossip. "I made a firm decision a few months ago not to gossip. God had shown me how badly I had damaged people with my mouth. I had little difficulty until I visited with a woman in my Sunday school class. Before I knew it, we were gossiping about another member. When I told her about my decision not to gossip, she laughed and told me that we weren't gossiping—we were just trying to understand the other member's problem. I don't think it is wise for me to spend time with her again unless we can agree not to gossip."

A Decision to Say No

In order for your friend to resist a temptation, she must make a firm decision to say no. With her, list the consequences of deliberate sin, such as guilt, separation from God, loss of joy, aloneness, hurting God, broken relationships, a heavy heart, and spiritual and physical death. Help her to look at what she has, rather than at what she doesn't have. Remind her that Satan always tries to tempt a person by telling them what they *can't* have or do. Help her to look instead at all the things she can have or do by following God's way.

Take Thoughts Captive

Second Corinthians 10:5 says to "refute arguments and theories and reasonings and every proud and lofty thing that sets itself up against the [true] knowledge of God; and . . . lead every thought and purpose away captive into the obedience of Christ."

We are free to choose our own thoughts. Just as we may sit in front of our television set and change channels, we can also change our thoughts. If your friend becomes captivated by thoughts, encourage her not only to pray and build her mind up with God's Word, but also to take action which will involve strong concentration.

One man who was dealing with temptation began jogging, because he said that the activity helped him clear his mind, as well as relieve physical tension. Getting outside, enjoying nature, helping someone else, or starting a new hobby will provide a focus for the mind, relieving the tendency to dwell on a temptation.

Receive God's Forgiveness for Past Failure and Go On

Help your friend accept God's forgiveness for her failures and to forgive others who may have been involved. Help her to determine not to look back, but to see herself as cleansed from the past (1 John 1:19; Philippians 3:13; also see chapter 12: "Guilt").

Recognize the Power of God

Encourage your friend to use thoughts of temptation as a cue to call upon God for help. Suggest that she memorize or write down specific verses that describe God's power in her. Some you might suggest are Ephesians 1:19; 3:20; 2 Timothy 1:7; and 2 Corinthians 4:7.

Teach your friend about the Holy Spirit within her.

First John 4:4 says, "He Who lives in you is greater (mightier) than he who is in the world." Help your friend call upon the power of the Holy Spirit within.

Be Alert and Pray

The Word tells us to be vigilant, for Satan roams around like a roaring lion, looking for someone whom he can destroy (1 Peter 5:8). Do not underestimate counterattacks Satan will bring upon God's children. Just because he may lose one battle does not mean that he will give up his desire to destroy your friend. Even though your friend has resisted him, expect Satan to return to attempt harm. We are told that following Jesus' temptation in the wilderness, "And when the devil had ended every [the complete cycle of] temptation, he [temporarily] left Him [that is, stood off from Him] until another more opportune and favorable time" (Luke 4:13).

Remind your friend of Satan's methods, and suggest that you pray together regularly for a specified period of time.

Stand Firm with Hope

The Holy Spirit is called our "Comforter (Counselor, Helper, Advocate, Intercessor, Strengthener, Standby)" (John 16:7). During your friend's struggle, stand by her. Ask her to call you at times when she experiences difficulty. Pray for God to give you encouraging words for her. Continue to assure her of God's love, as well as your own. Remember that when temptation comes, we have all the power of heaven on our side to resist. And:

For because He Himself [in His humanity] has suffered in being tempted (tested and tried), He is able [immedi-

261

ately] to run to the cry of (assist, relieve) those who are being tempted and tested and tried [and who therefore are being exposed to suffering]. (Hebrews 2:18)

LIFE APPLICATIONS ———————————

1. Have you ever felt the "pull" of temptation toward a sin? What was it like?

2. What are some areas in which you are most vulnerable to temptation?

3. Are there times of the day, month, or year when you are more vulnerable to certain temptations? What are they?

4. Have you ever felt that you "deserved" to have or do something that was not good for you? What?

5. Have you ever tried to "build up credit" with God in one area so that you could justify a sin in another area?

6. How can you approach another Christian whom you believe is involved in a sin?

7. How can you become confident about your decision to approach that person?

8. Has there been a time when you were tempted and God provided an "escape route" for you? When?

9. Have you ever been so tempted that you could not overcome without the help of someone else's prayers on your behalf?

10. Read John 10:10.

PART THREE

THE STEADFAST HEART

16

HOW TO PERSEVERE THROUGH THE PROBLEM

And let us not lose heart and grow weary and faint in
acting nobly and doing right, for in due time and
at the appointed season we shall reap. . . .
GALATIANS 6:9

I don't feel that I'm helping my friend very much. Nothing seems to help!"

"John has so many problems! When one situation is resolved, five more problems appear! Sometimes I wish I'd
never gotten involved!"

It was the end of a long week, and I was tired. Each
person who had come into my office had been in extreme
pain—impossible situations, hurtful relationships, pain
from the past. I felt overwhelmed by the sheer size and
number of the problems! Why, I wondered, had I ever

wanted to be a counselor? I felt so inadequate and weary. I wanted to give up.

As you help people in pain, sometimes you will feel like giving up. You will encounter those who seem to have one crisis after another, those whose problems seem to last forever, and those whose concerns appear unsolvable. How can *you* stay encouraged? How can you support someone else when you feel inadequate yourself? How do you stand with your friend until her problem is resolved? In this chapter, you will find ways to stay encouraged and to persevere, so that you won't "lose heart and grow weary and faint" (Galatians 6:9).

Count the Cost

If we don't consider the demands and "costs" that may be required, it will be easy to lose heart.

It is such a thrill to watch my husband, Wayne, cross the finish line of a marathon. The crowds cheer. *Chariots of Fire* is played over the loudspeakers. I see his tired, but triumphant, smile as he completes the 26.2 miles of the course.

In the thrill of the moment, I imagine myself completing a marathon, receiving my medal, and feeling the exhilaration of success. Then I remember the mornings when Wayne rises at 5:00 A.M. to run twenty miles; the way he watches his weight and maintains a diet designed to build strength; the books he reads on training and equipment; all the long hours he spends preparing to run in a race.

Suddenly, my momentary dream is replaced by a dose of reality. I have to admit it. I want the glory of completing a marathon, but I don't want to pay the price required to do it!

Jesus instructs us that to persevere, we should consider the cost before beginning:

> Whoever does not persevere and carry his own cross and come after (follow) Me cannot be My disciple. For which of you, wishing to build a farm building, does not first sit down and calculate the cost [to see] whether he has sufficient means to finish it? Otherwise, when he has laid the foundation and is unable to complete [the building], all who see it will begin to mock and jeer at him, saying, This man began to build and was not able (worth enough) to finish. (Luke 14:27–30)

Before you are tempted to quit, remind yourself of the possible costs involved in counseling which you examined before you began. Costs may include postponing preferred tasks in order to be with your friend, listening when you are tired, being inconvenienced, and disciplining yourself to pray, study, or read. You can never predict all the "costs," but by recognizing that there will be responsibility and sacrifice needed, you will be better able to persevere with your friend through the problem.

"As you help people in pain, sometimes you will feel like giving up."

Set Short-term Goals

Sighing, I tell Wayne of my decision not to run a marathon. Agreeing that running a marathon might not be a reasonable goal (since I can't even run a mile), he suggests that I might begin by walking. He reminds me that before he ever thought of running marathons, he started by running three miles, then training for 5K races to slowly increase his distances and his endurance. He encourages me to set some short-term goals, ones I can attain, and to slowly work up to a greater goal.

Once you decide that you want to help others, you may expect the success to be instantaneous! Sadly, most problems were created over long periods of time; their solutions will also involve time and patience.

When you are tempted to be discouraged, remind yourself that your friend's problems will not disappear overnight. In fact, you may never see them completely resolved! Ask God to help you set short-term goals with your friend, so that both of you will stay encouraged.

Develop the habit of dividing large tasks and solutions into manageable bits. For example, if you are encouraging a friend with a weight-loss program, don't set a goal of five pounds in one week. Set small goals that have a high probability of being reached quickly or she—and you—will be overwhelmed.

Learn from Your Mistakes

After a race, I watch Wayne replay each mile, looking for ways he can improve his performance. He catalogs each mistake in his mind, planning what he will do differently the next time. Rather than berating himself for any mistakes, he uses them to prepare for his next challenge.

It is inevitable that you will make a mistake with your friend. You may say the wrong thing at the wrong time, you may offend her, or you may find your suggestions were not helpful. Instead of being alarmed and discouraged, admit your mistake, apologize to your friend, see how you can prevent similar errors, and make a plan for next time. Mistakes can be great teachers, if we will let them work for us. Accept the fact that you will make mistakes. The important thing is to learn from your mistakes and keep on going!

Teaching a Sunday school class of preschoolers for the first time, Richard was apprehensive. "I really got myself into trouble at first," he reported. "In an effort to have them like me, I let them do whatever they wanted. Boy, was that a mistake! I learned very quickly what *not* to do!"

Paul shared his secret on keeping on:

> . . . but one thing I do [it is my one aspiration]: forgetting what lies behind and straining forward to what lies ahead, I press on toward the goal to win the [supreme and heavenly] prize to which God in Christ Jesus is calling us upward. (Philippians 3:13–14)

Principles of Perseverance

If anyone in the Bible had reason to give up, it was Moses. Moses seemed to have an impossible task—to lead the Israelites out of Egypt after 430 years of slavery. Moses started out with six hundred thousand men, in addition to at least that many women and children (Exodus 12:37). Can you imagine being in charge of over six hundred thousand people?

The book of Exodus chronicles the story of Moses and the problems he encountered with this nation. Moses must have experienced numerous and major disappointments with these people, but he persevered through forty years in the wilderness with a disobedient group of God's children. The principles God showed Moses and the children of Israel will help you persevere, too.

Remember God's Blessings and His Past Faithfulness

When situations become difficult, it is easy to become discouraged. Remembering past blessings and God's past faithfulness to you will help you persevere through the hard times.

To encourage the children of Israel, God gave specific observances to remind them of His past faithfulness. The Passover celebration, for example, was to be celebrated each year in the month of Abib (March-April) to remind Israel of its deliverance from Egypt. Each year, they were instructed to tell their children the story of God's deliverance, passing it down from generation to generation (Exodus 13:1–18). The observance of the Sabbath as a day of rest was also instituted as a means of remembering the Lord. The Lord told Moses:

> Say to the Israelites, Truly you shall keep My Sabbaths, for it is a sign between Me and you throughout your generations, that you may know that I, the Lord, sanctify you [set you apart for Myself]. (Exodus 31:13)

When you feel discouraged about the help you are giving to a friend or about your own situation, remind yourself of God's accomplishments.

A woman who started her own business told the following story. "When I first began my business, I relied on a small amount of money I had saved in order to get through the first several months.

"In January, however, all my savings was gone, and I had to depend totally on what I collected from my clients. When I received two large unexpected bills during those first weeks, I panicked. Where would the money come from? I could only trust that God would provide the needed money.

Then and in the months following, I was amazed to watch God provide the very amounts of money I needed, regardless of the size of my expenses. Not one month went by without my needs being met by God in some way.

I briefly forgot God's faithfulness, however, one month when I received an electric bill that was twice the amount I had expected! My faith plummeted! What was I to do? Where would the money be found? Suddenly, I remembered! God had been faithful to me all these months. Why did I think He would change? Was He trustworthy or not? Instantly, my mind cleared. He had been faithful to me in the past, and He would take care of this problem. The needed money came that month . . . and the next . . . and the next.

When you are tempted to give up, remember 1 Thessalonians 5:24:

> Faithful is He Who is calling you [to Himself] and utterly trustworthy, and He will also do it [fulfill His call by hallowing and keeping you].

Watch What You Say to Yourself

Each time a problem arose, the children of Israel began to whine! After God had delivered them from Pharaoh, it was no time before they forgot His promise, complaining when Pharaoh's army began chasing them (Exodus 14:10). When they came to a place where the drinking water was bitter, instead of looking for other water sources, they began to murmur and complain (Exodus 15:22–24). They acted as if each problem was a new opportunity to gripe!

If you allow yourself to complain, it won't be long until

you believe what you say! Then, instead of moving on to solve the problem, you will have created a new problem!

I once became very burdened and fatigued as I counseled a friend through a trying time. After several months of stressful events after which no solutions seemed to come, I found myself saying, "I don't know if things will ever get any better!" or "It looks as if there isn't a good solution!"

A friend confronted me one day with my discouraging talk. "You need to watch what you say in front of yourself. You're about to talk your faith away!" I realized she was right. I was actually convincing myself that my continued counsel was useless, and, as a result, my commitment to my friend was waning.

Say to Yourself What God Says

After my friend confronted me, I began to say things, such as, "I know that God is faithful. He gives strength for all things. With Him, nothing is impossible," and "God is our help in every time of trouble. He knows the future and He will provide." As I heard myself speak the *truth* of the Word of God my faith grew. I was able to continue to help my friend through her difficulties.

After God delivered the children of Israel from the Egyptians through the miracle at the Red Sea, Moses and the Israelites sang a song to the Lord that recounted the event and praised His mighty strength and deliverance (Exodus 15:1–21). Their song was passed down through the generations of Israel and served as a continual encouragement of God's Word, works, and faithfulness to them.

When you encounter an "impossible" situation, ask God for His perspective. Find Scripture that addresses the needs of your friend. Repeat His words to yourself and to your friend.

"If you allow yourself to complain, it won't be long until you believe what you say!"

If the problem concerns worry about the future, for example, you might want to repeat Jeremiah 29:11, "For I know the thoughts and plans that I have for you, says the Lord, thoughts and plans for welfare and peace and not for evil, to give you hope in your final outcome," or Psalm 31:14–15, "You are my God. My times are in Your hands."

Don't forget to study God's Word for application in your own life. When you are helping others, it is easy to let your Bible study revolve around your friend's needs. If you fill your mind with His Word during the easier times, you will be able to recall it more easily during the difficult ones.

A Bible teacher related, "I realized that I've been spending all of my study time preparing for my classes. I can't remember the last time I sat down with my Bible and opened it just for myself! I forgot how much I need strength from God's Word, too."

Pour Out Your Heart to God

When you feel like giving up, pour out your heart to God. The book of Exodus recounts one of the many instances in which the children of Israel complained to Moses about their situation:

> . . . but there was no water for the people to drink. Therefore, the people contended with Moses, and said,

Give us water that we may drink. And Moses said to them, Why do you find fault with me? Why do you tempt the Lord and try His patience? But the people thirsted there for water, and the people murmured against Moses, and said, Why did you bring us up out of Egypt to kill us and our children and livestock with thirst? (Exodus 17:1–3)

Can you imagine Moses' exasperation? He must have been tempted to leave them and their complaints to find some other way to serve God. Perseverance must have been a tough choice!

Instead of giving up, "Moses cried to the Lord, What shall I do with this people? They are almost ready to stone me" (Exodus 17:4). He poured out his frustration to God, and God gave him a plan. He answered the need by providing water from a rock!

In times of discouragement, tell God how you are feeling. Give Him your frustration and doubt and fears. Remember, He is the God who brings water out of rocks!

Take Action

When you pour out your heart to God, and if He gives you an instruction, take action! When the children of Israel were camped by the Red Sea, they saw the Egyptians chasing them. There was nowhere to go! They became frightened and cried out to God, so God had Moses tell them to quit being afraid because He would rescue them (Exodus 14:9–14). After God had assured them, they still continued to cry, so God told Moses, "Why do you cry to Me? Tell the people of Israel to go forward!" (Exodus 14:15). It was time to quit praying and get moving! Taking action will help you to persevere until the problem is resolved.

Trust God with the Outcome

As He leads, keep your eyes on Him, not the problem. Look at the final outcome, not at the obstacles.

Remember That God Has Control

When tragedies occur or difficulties seem to compound and continue endlessly, it is easy to forget that God is all-powerful. We often think we know just what God should do, or exactly how He ought to work out a situation. When things don't happen the way we thought they would, we easily lose heart and doubt God.

In the midst of a long and difficult crisis, we must face the fact that sometimes life on the earth is awfully tough, even with God's help. It was hard for Jesus, and it will be hard for us. Jesus reminds us, "In the world you have tribulation and trials and distress and frustration; but be of good cheer [take courage; be confident, certain, undaunted]! For I have overcome the world. [I have deprived it of power to harm you and have conquered it for you]" (John 16:33).

Look at the Things Not Seen

Paul encountered obstacle after obstacle as he preached to the Gentiles. He was shipwrecked, beaten, put in jail, left for dead several times, forgotten, and persecuted. Had he looked at the outward circumstances or immediate results, he could have easily been dissuaded from God's calling. Paul, however, saw his situations from a loftier perspective, and was able to write:

> Therefore, we do not become discouraged (utterly spirit-less, exhausted, and wearied out through fear). Though our outer man is [progressively] decaying and wasting

275

away, yet our inner self is being [progressively] renewed day after day. For our light, momentary affliction (this slight distress of the passing hour) is ever more and more abundantly preparing and producing and achieving for us an everlasting weight of glory. . . . *Since we consider and look not to the things that are seen but to the things that are unseen; for the things that are visible are temporal (brief and fleeting), but the things that are invisible are deathless and everlasting.* (2 Corinthians 4:16–18, emphasis added)

Ask God to help you have His eyes as you view difficulties. He knows the outcome, and He is in control.

My heart was heavy as a young woman left my office. Her distress and remorse over her abortion were painful to watch. I had listened and prayed with her, but I felt so inadequate to heal her hurt. Only God could help her, but I so wanted to offer her His encouragement. When she didn't keep her next appointment, I was concerned. Unable to reach her by telephone, I wrote her a note. Still no word from her.

Several months later I ran into her.

"How are you doing?" I asked.

Her face broke into a smile. She said, "I've been so much better. Talking with you that day made all the difference. God used your words that day to give me strength and hope. I have experienced so much healing, and I'm really beginning to know His love. Thank you so much for being there for me!"

I was stunned. I couldn't remember anything I had said that day, but God knew what she had needed to hear, and He had done the work. He engineered her circumstances as well as the final outcome. In spite of the situation or my opinion of it, God is sovereign, and He will perform His will!

Remember that the battle is in the spiritual realm. You will not always know the forces at work in a situation. But God knows. His Word will accomplish what He purposes, and He knows the final outcome! As you help a friend, remember you are one of God's links of healing. You may not see the entire picture or be aware of the final outcome, but you can trust Him with the outcome and be available for Him to use as part of the process.

Eternal Rewards

When you are tempted to give up because you don't see immediate results, consider the eternal rewards.

Let God Reward You

Colossians 3:23–24 says:

> Whatever may be your task, work at it heartily (from the soul), as [something done] for the Lord and not for men. Knowing [with all certainty] that it is from the Lord [and not from men] that you will receive the inheritance which is your [real] reward.

Scripture tells us that God also rewards us for perseverance:

> Blessed (happy, to be envied) is the man who is patient under trial and stands up under temptation, for when he has stood the test and been approved, he will receive [the victor's] crown of life which God has promised to those who love Him. (James 1:12)

I have fought the good (worthy, honorable, and noble) fight, I have finished the race, I have kept (firmly held) the faith. [As to what remains] henceforth there is laid up for me the [victor's] crown of righteousness [for being right with God and doing right], which the Lord, the righteous Judge, will award to me and recompense me on that [great] day—and not to me only, but also to all those who have loved and yearned for and welcomed His appearing (His return). (2 Timothy 4:7–8)

Remember Heaven

When you are tempted to give up, to grow weary, or to lose heart, remind yourself of these words from the book of Revelation. Jesus is described as:

clothed with a robe which reached to His feet and with a girdle of gold about His breast. His head and His hair were white like white wool, [as white] as snow, and His eyes [flashed] like a flame of fire. His feet glowed like burnished (bright) bronze as it is refined in a furnace, and His voice was like the sound of many waters. (Revelation 1:13–15)

The New Jerusalem, prepared for the believers is described as:

Clothed in God's glory [in all its splendor and radiance]. The luster of it resembled a rare and most precious jewel, like jasper, shining clear as crystal. . . . The wall was built of jasper, while the city [itself was of] pure gold, clear and transparent like glass. The foundation [stones] of the wall of the city were ornamented with all of the precious stones. The first foundation [stone] was jasper, the second sapphire, the third chalcedony (or white agate), the fourth emerald, the fifth onyx, the sixth sardius,

278

the seventh chrysolite, the eighth beryl, the ninth topaz, the tenth chrysoprase, the eleventh jacinth, the twelfth amethyst. (Revelation 21:11, 18–20)

In this heaven, God "will live (encamp, tent) among them; and they shall be His people, and God shall personally be with them and be their God. God will wipe away every tear from their eyes; and death shall be no more, neither shall there be anguish (sorrow and mourning) nor grief nor pain any more . . ." (Revelation 21:3–4).

So, ". . . let us not lose heart and grow weary and faint in acting nobly and doing right, for in due time and at the appointed season we shall reap . . ." (Galatians 6:9).

LIFE APPLICATIONS ————————————

1. Have you ever just wanted to give up on helping another person? Have you ever felt too tired to listen anymore or to care anymore? What did you do that helped? What did you do that didn't help?

2. What are some of the "costs" you have experienced when you were involved in helping a friend?

3. Share a time when you had a large task to complete or goal to accomplish. How did you break it down into obtainable, short-term goals? Did this keep you encouraged?

4. Recall a time when you felt discouraged. Were you able to remind yourself of God's past faithfulness to you? What did this do to your level of discouragement?

5. Do you feel you can tell God *everything* you feel? Or are you only comfortable telling God your good feelings? Recall a time when you "poured out your heart" to God. What was the result?

6. What have others done for you that has been encouraging? What helps you the most when you are discouraged?

7. What keeps you going? What are your rewards for perseverance? What are God's rewards for those who persevere?

8. Can you remember how you felt when you crossed a "finish line," met a deadline, or when a goal had been reached? Describe in one word your feeling at that time.

17

THE DIMENSION OF SPIRITUAL WARFARE

Put on God's whole armor . . . that you may be able
successfully to stand up against . . . the devil.
EPHESIANS 6:11

Would you deliberately go into physical combat without weapons? Of course not! However, many Christians enter into territory which Satan has claimed as his own, ignorant of and unarmed for the battle which will occur.

In our modern, rational, scientific world, it is difficult for many to believe there is an actual person named Satan in command of evil spirits which assail us daily. Scripture, however, far from ignoring these powers, boldly unveils and describes them. Evil is very real in this world, and the Bible warns the believer not to underestimate Satan's ability to defeat us. Paul describes our mortal struggle with the evil realm of the spirit world:

For we are not wrestling with flesh and blood [contending only with physical opponents], but against the despotisms, against the powers, against [the master spirits who are] the world rulers of this present darkness, against the spirit forces of wickedness in the heavenly (supernatural) sphere. (Ephesians 6:12)

A pastor friend told me of his experience with Holly, a ten-year-old child who had been sexually and physically abused by both her parents and later by foster parents. She was very depressed, withdrawn, and volatile. One day as he was working with her, her face contorted and her eyes blazed. Suddenly, a strange, deep voice came out of her mouth saying, "I hate you. I won't leave her, and you can't make me!" He was stunned. Holly's countenance had changed completely. The word *evil* swept through his mind, and he shuddered. Although he didn't realize it at the time, he was in the presence of an evil spirit which was acting through that little child.

Throughout the Gospels, Jesus confronted demonic forces of darkness, casting them out and freeing men and women from oppression. When He sent the disciples out two by two on their first mission, He gave them power and authority over evil spirits. As Jesus prepared to leave the earth, He told them again, "Go into all the world and preach and publish openly the good news (the Gospel) to every creature. . . . And these attesting signs will accompany those who believe: *in My name they will drive out demons . . .*" (Mark 16:15, 17, emphasis added). As disciples also of Jesus today, our mission is still the same. As you work with friends who are hurting, you will see firsthand the destructive forces of Satan. Therefore, it is essential that we understand Satan, how he works, and his defeat so that we may, with Jesus, begin to undo the works the devil has done in their lives (1 John 3:8).

Who Is Satan? Who Are Evil Spirits?

Bible scholars believe that Satan was, at one time, the chief angel in heaven who chose to attempt to usurp God. He led a futile revolt against God, and, along with other angelic followers, was cast out of heaven. Because God created Satan, the power Satan has over the world is limited.

Evil spirits are those fallen angels who joined Satan in his rebellion against God. Today they exist under Satan's command, and he uses them in attempts to carry out his purpose—to cause rebellion against God.

How Does Satan Work?

Although evil spirits are created beings and as such, are limited, nonetheless they are able to exert real power to directly afflict people or work through them. Just as God's love is expressed through our physical bodies, Satan also uses people in his attempt to accomplish his evil purposes.

A therapist at a mental health clinic related her experience working with a young woman who had been emotionally abused as a child. "Sally could not trust others, God, or herself. As we worked together, we developed a good relationship, but she continued to think she was unworthy, unlovable, and unwanted—all of the lies Satan had led her to believe about herself.

"One night about three o'clock in the morning, I heard a pounding on my door. Sally was yelling for me to let her in. When I didn't immediately do so, she became enraged and began firing shots at the house. I was terrified. For three hours, she sat outside my house, at times silent, at times shouting. I had no idea what would happen.

"Although her actions caused me great alarm and fear, I knew *her* intent was not to harm me. I didn't know much about the activity of Satan then, but I realized that it was not this woman who was trying to frighten and harass me, but evil spirits working through her."

Galatians 5:22–23 tells us the fruit of the Holy Spirit is love, joy, peace, patience, kindness, goodness, faithfulness, gentleness, and self-control. Satan rejoices when he can cause people, especially Christians, to act in hatred, selfishness, strife, cruelty, envy, or to act out of wrong motives.

While evil spirits of Satan use physical bodies through which to act or afflict, they also work through *circumstances* to hinder God's purposes.

Recently, a friend received a gift of money to be used by her and her husband to go out of town for the weekend together. This present from God was perfectly timed. She was exhausted from her work as a student and part-time employee, in addition to caring for her husband and three children. She had a solid marriage, but having little time together or the money to get away was beginning to hurt the relationship.

Upon receiving the gift, she immediately began to make plans to get away for a weekend. Every obstacle imaginable seemed to arise—her mother couldn't keep the children, her son appeared to be coming down with chicken pox, and the woman who was substituting for her at work became ill. She almost gave up! The circumstances seemed to be overwhelming!

She and her husband did get away for the weekend—at a beautiful and usually expensive resort that just happened to have a special weekend rate that weekend *only!* The oppression that she had felt lifted. She returned home refreshed in mind, body, and spirit. Satan tried to rob her of God's blessing for her and her husband through a series of circumstances.

Can a Christian Be Possessed by Satan or Evil Spirits?

I do not believe that a Christian can be *possessed* by Satan or by his spirits. Strictly speaking, the word *possession* denotes a state of being owned or controlled. When a person is possessed, someone or something else has power over her. A Christian, who has been born again by the blood of Jesus Christ, is "stamped with the seal of the long-promised Holy Spirit" (Ephesians 1:13), and as a result, cannot be possessed by a spirit of Satan. That seal upon the Christian is God's Spirit "in our hearts as the security deposit and guarantee" (2 Corinthians 1:22) of our new life. We are owned by God forever, purchased with the price of Jesus' blood for our eternal salvation.

"Oppression is a heaviness, a weight, a feeling of not quite being yourself."

I do believe, however, that a Christian can be *oppressed* by evil spirits. To *oppress* means to lie heavily on the mind, or to weigh down. Some have described the state of being oppressed as "having a black cloud over their minds."

Oppression is a heaviness, a weight, a feeling of not

quite being yourself. Satan can confuse, torment, and hurt Christians; but he cannot "own" them. The Bible tells us that Satan "roams around like a lion roaring [in fierce hunger], seeking someone to seize upon and devour" (1 Peter 5:8). All Christians are targets of Satan because he hates God and he hates us.

How Does Satan Oppress Christians?

As Jesus taught, the work of Satan is to kill, steal, and destroy, while the work of Jesus is to give us a full and abundant life (John 10:10). Satan wants to rob us of this abundant relationship with our Father, halt the spread of the Gospel of Jesus Christ, destroy our families and health, endanger our safety, steal our hope, and eventually destroy our faith in Jesus.

Satan works through deception and lies. Jesus described Satan as "the father of lies and all that is false" (John 8:44). As you work with others, you need to be aware of some of the faces Satan wears.

Fear

Satan sends spirits of fear to Christians in order to hinder them in God's purposes for them.

Several years ago, I was preparing to leave on a trip during which I would be speaking about child abuse. The night before I was to depart, I awoke around two o'clock in the morning, gripped with terror. There was an evil darkness hovering over my bed. Its presence was so vivid that I could not have been more aware of it had it actually been visible. I was terrified, because it was so frightening and oppressive. I knew that Satan had come to disturb me, torment me, and make me ineffective on my trip.

Obsessions and Condemnation

Satan also uses recurring thoughts of condemnation or other deceptions to torment Christians.

"Satan sends spirits of fear to Christians in order to hinder them in God's purposes for them."

Cindy was an attractive, vivacious young woman who had always believed that whatever she did wasn't "good enough." She continually criticized herself for what she said or didn't say, her behavior, and her appearance. She analyzed others' reactions toward her, always concluding the worst about herself. Several days after I prayed for her to be delivered from spirits of condemnation and obsessive thinking she wrote:

> I can't tell you what it means to me to have been delivered from the evil spirits that oppressed me since I was a little child! I never dreamed help could be so close! I thought I had been living in the Spirit, but I was really just struggling in the flesh. I condemned myself for everything! When I left a meeting at church, I replayed everything I had said. Was it the right thing? Did I look stupid? Did I offend anyone? I always found something to condemn in myself! I lived in fear and dread most of the time.
>
> When I learned about the authority I have as a believer

in Christ to use the name of Jesus against Satan, it made all the difference! I thought *I* had been condemning myself! When I realized that the condemnation was coming from an evil power outside of myself, and that God had given me the power to make it leave, my whole life changed!

I can see now that, not only did the blood of Jesus give me salvation, it also gave me deliverance from evil! I *know* now that there is no condemnation for me (Romans 8:1)!

I experienced the reality of this for the first time recently when I really did make a stupid remark. As I was driving home from that encounter, I almost condemned myself, but when I did, I felt God's hand on me. So, instead of feeling that I must condemn myself, I was able to laugh and say, "That's okay, Cindy! That may have been stupid, but I'm not going to condemn you for it!"

Physical Torment

Now Jesus was teaching in one of the synagogues on the Sabbath. And there was a woman there who for eighteen years had had an infirmity caused by a spirit (a demon of sickness). She was bent completely forward and utterly unable to straighten herself up or to look upward. And when Jesus saw her, He called [her to Him] and said to her, Woman, you are released from your infirmity! Then He laid [His] hands on her, and instantly she was made straight, and she recognized and thanked and praised God. (Luke 13:10–13)

Satan oppresses Christians with physical problems, as well as with addictions and other behaviors which cause physical torment and distress. Many say, "Well, heart disease runs in the family." While it is true that we may be predisposed to certain conditions in our bodies, many times

Satan will oppress families with diseases and conditions. When we are unaware of this strategy, we are more likely to accept the problem as something we have no power over. This is not always the case.

Family Disturbances

Satan loves to divide families and to create chaos in Christian homes. Unreconciled problems with spouses or with children are probably one of the most frequent complaints heard. Sometimes these family disturbances are due to oppression from evil spirits. This was the case with the Randolph family. As Mr. Randolph observed:

> I always knew there was evil in the world, but I didn't think it was possible for it to affect Christian homes as it did mine! I really couldn't understand it when our fourteen-year-old daughter refused to sleep on her bed. I thought it was some sort of phase she was going through. Then she brought a wooden cross into her bedroom, said she had to sleep on the floor with the cross in a certain position, or else she couldn't rest. When she began avoiding the family and arguing with her mother and me, I knew something was wrong. Our sweet, talkative, friendly daughter had turned into someone we hardly recognized!
>
> When you told us to pray over her room and to tell any spirits not of God to leave, I thought that was a little dramatic, but by this time, we were willing to try anything. We began praying over her room, praying for her, and asking our friends to pray that any evil spirits that were trying to attack our family be stopped.
>
> The first week was about the same. Then we began to notice changes. Within two months, we had our daughter back! That convinced me of the seriousness of the battle we, as Christians, are in!

289

Addictions

What more evil way to enslave a person, to make a person feel condemned and unloved by God, to create doubt and havoc in a life than through an addiction!

Carolyn's story typifies this problem:

> I was thirty-seven-years old, and unhappily married with three children, when I finally admitted to myself that I had become an alcoholic. During the previous six months, the Lord had drawn me back to Himself and established me in a small body of loving, caring believers. Together we had experienced many miracles of rebirth, healing, and deliverance, yet I continued to wrestle with alcohol. Each day I promised God that I would not drink, yet every night I broke my promise. My guilt, remorse, and self-loathing tormented me, but I failed to find the strength within myself to give up alcohol entirely. I wanted so much to present my body as a living sacrifice, yet I was constantly defeated!

The Weapons of Our Warfare

Second Corinthians 10:4 tells us that "the weapons of our warfare are not physical [weapons of flesh and blood], but they are mighty before God . . ." As you work with others, remember that the Father has "delivered and drawn us to Himself out of the control and the dominion of darkness and has transferred us into the kingdom of the Son of His love" (Colossians 1:13) and that God, in the person of the Holy Spirit, has given believers power over the devil and all of his works (1 John 4:4). As you work with those who may be oppressed by Satan and his evil spirits, you will need to know the weapons available to you that are "mighty before

God for the overthrow and destruction of strongholds" (2 Corinthians 10:4).

The Name of Jesus

Lying in my bed that night, frightened by the oppressive presence in my room, I realized I should pray, but I was so startled I couldn't think of anything to pray! Suddenly a song I hadn't heard in years came to my mind, as clearly as if it were being sung to me. The words implanted themselves in my mind:

> In the name of Jesus, In the name of Jesus,
>   we have the victory!
> In the name of Jesus, In the name of Jesus,
>   demons will have to flee!

Of course! The name of Jesus! God reminded me that all power and authority are given to the believer in that Name (Philippians 2:9–10). I began to say aloud, "In the name of Jesus, I command you to leave me now!" As I repeated this command several times, I began to gradually sense the evil presence withdraw from my room. I was able to go back to sleep and get the rest I needed for my trip. Satan and his spirits cannot stand the name of Jesus.

Our Armor

In Ephesians 6:11, we are commanded to "put on God's whole armor." Although our weapons are invisible, they are the most powerful weapons in the universe. Daily, it is important that we check our equipment—to see that each part is in place and in "working order."

The Belt of Truth. Each morning you need to tighten the belt of truth. Since one of Satan's most powerful weapons is falsehood or lies, it is important to stay girded with God's Word. When circumstances arise that could deceive or confuse you, God's truth will reign in your mind, and you will not be swayed, nor will you stumble. When you are dealing with a specific problem, make sure that you know what God says about it in Scripture.

The Breastplate of Righteousness. The breastplate of righteousness is placed over your heart to protect your emotions. Satan will accuse us saying, "Who are you to be fighting this battle? You've sinned so many times and made so many mistakes! Who do you think you are?" When this happens, remember that you *are* the righteousness of Christ (2 Corinthians 5:21), you are totally approved by God (John 6:27), and He Himself has ordained your position in His army (Ephesians 6:10–18). Do not be intimidated. The battle has nothing to do with your own righteousness or power, but everything to do with Christ who lives in you! Tell Satan, "I rebuke you, Satan, in the name of Jesus Christ! I know that in my own flesh I have no power, but the One who has all power lives inside of me. Therefore, through Him, I have overcome!"

The Gospel of Peace. We are told in Ephesians 6:15 to "shod your feet" with the gospel of peace. When you approach the enemy, it may be tempting to run, but remember, as a believer, Jesus has given you His own peace (John 14:27). When you are filled with peace, you need not fear adversity because you will be stable, calm, and sure-footed. As others see God help you to walk through difficulties, you will have opportunities to witness for Him.

The Shield of Faith. You can protect yourself from the darts of Satan by keeping the shield of faith raised before you. Your shield of faith is composed of knowing God's

Word, remembering the many times He has delivered you in the past, and continually giving thanks that He is with you. Especially when things happen that you do not understand, depend on His Word, remember, and rejoice!

The Helmet of Salvation. Just as the breastplate of righteousness protects your heart, the helmet of salvation will protect your mind. Remember that no power, person, or circumstance can touch you without your Father's permission, because you are His! Although it may seem as if Satan is winning, always remember that God has the victory already won for you! Because of our salvation, we do not even have to fear death, because Jesus conquered death for us. We are saved now, and we will still be saved in the life hereafter.

The Sword of the Spirit. The sword of the Spirit, our one offensive weapon, is God's Word. When you speak His Word, God promises that It will accomplish Its purpose (Isaiah 55:11). When you feel under pressure, be careful not to "talk yourself" into a corner so that Satan can trap you. Absorb God's Word and speak it to yourself often. Address the enemy with Scripture, and God will overcome him with power.

The Prayer of Deliverance

When the time comes for you to pray with your friend for deliverance from evil spirits, there are several points to be carefully considered.

Honesty. As clearly as you can, determine the intensity of your friend's desire to be free from Satan's power over her. Ask her if she is ready to turn from temptation related to past sin in that area. Does she desire to follow Jesus the rest of her life, or does she just desire freedom from fear and torment?

If you are uncertain of her salvation, be sure that she is already born again by the spirit of Christ, and ask her to pray, entrusting herself entirely into the hands of Jesus.

Humility. It is important for her to recognize and to confess that she cannot free herself, and is totally dependent upon God.

Repentance. Help your friend identify personal sins which may have opened the door for oppression. If she is willing, ask her to confess them to God and to ask His forgiveness for those and any other sins that come to her mind.

Forgiveness. In order to receive the blessing of deliverance from God, your friend will need to forgive those who have harmed her (see chapter 11: "Bitterness").

Identify the Spirits. Before you pray with someone to be delivered from evil spirits, it is important to identify those spirits. You might ask, "In what area do you feel the most oppressed?" "What feelings or behaviors bother you the most?" There are specific spirits whom Satan sends to oppress us. Some of the most common ones are lust, illness, fear, greed, insanity, condemnation, guilt, discouragement, deception, murder, suicide, anger, depression, and addiction.

Prayer. When you begin your prayer time, thank God for His presence with you. Pray to be filled with God's Holy Spirit, as well as to be equipped with the gift of discerning the spirits. During the prayer time, continue to be open to identifying other spirits that may not have been named or recognized. The gift of discernment (1 Corinthians 12:10) is one gift of the Spirit which God will use to help you in this. If you sense the influence of a spirit but cannot name it, ask God and wait for His guidance. Ask God to protect you and your friend.

Renounce Satan and His Spirits. Ask your friend to renounce every spirit which has oppressed her. For example, if she has been involved in sexual sins, ask her to renounce the spirit of lust in the name of Jesus. If she has been afflicted with illness which does not respond to traditional methods of treatment, ask her to renounce the spirit of affliction.

As your friend renounces each spirit, pray with her, speaking the truth of God's Word. Ask the Holy Spirit to cleanse her entire being of the effects of evil. After you and your friend have finished renouncing the evil spirits, pray that God will fill her with His Holy Spirit and heal her from the damage that Satan has caused in her inner self, as well as in her life.

Praise and Thanksgiving. As your friend is set free, always remember to praise God for the power of His Spirit who performs mighty acts of deliverance! Thank Him for loving her enough to come with compassion and mercy to set your friend free. Thank Him for His power within you that made you able to stand!

The rest of Carolyn's story is a testimony to that power.

When I began to realize I couldn't successfully overcome my addiction to alcohol, God brought to my attention books and tapes attesting that forces in the world called evil spirits cause us to do things we really don't want to do. Furthermore, I learned that the evil spirits who tormented even children of God could be bound or cast away, just as Jesus had done during His earthly ministry! What good news that was to me! I immediately began to seek for this deliverance and, on a night of the Lord's choosing, I was delivered from the spirit of alcohol and all the bondages that accompany it through the prayers and commands of fellow believers.

Since that evening in March 1970, I have never had any desire to drink or smoke. I have learned to maintain and build on this deliverance by avoiding old lifestyles, listening to certain music, reading some books, and breaking away from specific old friendships which could draw my thoughts and actions back to my old way of living.

I learned to live in praise and thanksgiving by saturating my thoughts with God's Word. Other trials and tests have come, but alcohol has never again been my problem!

How to Keep Alert

There are certain times that you will be more likely to be attacked by Satan and his spirits. Knowing what to do and how to prevent attack will protect you.

Doing the Works of Jesus

"The reason the Son of God was made manifest (visible) was to undo (destroy, loosen, and dissolve) the works the devil [has done]" (1 John 3:8). Satan is furious when his purposes are thwarted. When you are beginning to do the works of Jesus, Satan will oppress you, trying to make you quit.

Giving in to Temptation

It is important to confess any sins which you have committed *daily*. You cannot hear God clearly unless you have a clear conscience, nor can you afford the distraction that sin brings.

Harboring Unforgiveness

Be sure that you hold nothing against anyone. Love and power cannot reign in your mind if anger and resentment are present.

Remember the Importance of Intercession

Often we believe that we are taking a more active part in battle if we are teaching, counseling, or witnessing. However, the most important and most powerful work you can do is to pray. When you earnestly pray for evil forces to be broken over your friend's life, you will be intensely involved. God's greatest works will directly follow your prayers. Because you have humbled yourself and turned to Him in quietness, He will move in ways you never imagined.

In order to provide godly counsel, you will need to find the mind of Christ in matters which concern your friend. There may be various solutions to your friend's problem, but it is only through prayer that you and she will find God's wisdom for her life. Only God knows the best way to draw her to Himself, and it is important to always remember that closeness to Him is top priority.

Pray Without Ceasing

Prayer is necessary for protection because Satan will constantly come against you and your friend. We are told to "pray at all times" and to "keep alert" (Ephesians 6:18).

Prayer will also keep you close to God. When you are alone and quiet with Him, you will hear His still, small voice assuring your heart of His love for you. He will assure you of His will and His ability to sustain you.

On the Battlefield

We have been amply supplied with all that we need to battle the forces of evil. As we stay near to our Father, He promises His complete armor and protection while we battle as His soldiers. God Himself has said:

> But no weapon that is formed against you shall prosper, and every tongue that shall rise against you in judgment you shall show to be in the wrong. This [peace, righteousness, security, triumph over oppression] is the heritage of the servants of the Lord. . . . (Isaiah 54:17)

LIFE APPLICATIONS _____

1. Do you believe that evil spirits exist? Why?

2. When did you first recognize the need for "spiritual warfare" against Satan?

3. Can you recall a time when Satan tried to keep you from following God's will?

4. Have you ever felt oppressed? How would you describe oppression?

5. If you have been oppressed, did you need the prayers of others before you were able to get relief?

6. What are the weapons of your warfare? What gifts of the Holy Spirit has God given through you?

7. Do you feel that you need to give more attention to Satan's efforts to harm?

8. In looking back, can you recall times when prayers and the knowledge of spiritual weapons would have prevented difficulties in your or someone else's life?

9. Have you prayed with anyone for deliverance from evil spirits? What are necessary steps involved?

10. Do you have a prayer partner?

18

THE IMPORTANCE OF CELEBRATION

Rejoice with those who rejoice [sharing others' joy].
ROMANS 12:15

*O*vercoming a problem, making a change, breaking a habit—all are causes for great celebration! The Word is full of moments of celebration. David danced with joy to celebrate the return of the Ark of the Lord (2 Samuel 6:14). God commanded the children of Israel to celebrate certain events, in remembrance of what He had done for them (Exodus 23:15–16; 34:18, 22). When the prodigal son returned, his father celebrated with a great feast (Luke 15:23).

On July 4, 1991, a celebration was held in honor of the Arkansans who had served in Operation Desert Storm. The air was filled with balloons, banners, and flags; sounds of patriotic music boomed; speeches were delivered with great gusto, and men and women in uniform proudly marched. All of us watched with tears of pride and joy as the crowd stood to sing "God Bless America," and a great wave of rejoicing rolled across the crowd at the end of the evening.

The feeling of victory was one to remember and to cherish. The men and women who had served our country left the stadium knowing their efforts had been recognized and appreciated! The celebration had accomplished its purpose.

As you go through a trial with your friend, you may not celebrate in a stadium with fireworks, but do take opportunities to celebrate her victories as God works. In this final chapter, we want to look at the why, the when, and the ways of celebration, so that you can "rejoice with those who rejoice" (Romans 12:15) with gusto!

Why Is Celebration Important?

Celebration praises God for His power and works, and it reinforces our confidence in Him to intervene in our lives.

With tears of joy, my friend Lori related, "I recently bought a house, and last night three friends gave me a housewarming party to celebrate my new home. Looking around the room at the people who had gathered, I was in awe. God has been so good to me! I have a beautiful home and friends who really care about me. How much He has done for me! He has intervened in my life, time and time again, and has brought these people into my life. I am overwhelmed with love and gratitude for His kindness and for these friends!"

Celebrations not only praise God, but also they honor your friend for her desire to follow Jesus and her ability to make decisions or take steps that have brought positive changes in her life by His power.

Lori continued, "As I opened the housewarming gifts, I

realized that the evening would never have occurred if I had not allowed Jesus to work in my life. Most of the people gathered were friends I had made because of my decision to follow Jesus. The party was not just a celebration of a new home, but for me, it was a celebration of a new way of life!"

"When the prodigal son returned, his father celebrated with a great feast."

Unfortunately, if victories are not celebrated, the disappointment may be all we recall years later. June told me, "When I completed one full year without taking a drink, I felt as if I had reached a landmark. I told my husband I would like to have a charm with the date of my one year anniversary engraved on it. I just knew he would get it for me, but he never did. My moment of glory passed with no recognition. He was the only person I knew whom I thought understood the importance of that one year mark. But he didn't come through. I've been sober for over twenty years, but that first year meant the most. I felt somehow robbed of some of my joy!"

Victories mean so much more when someone else celebrates them too! Celebration is important!

When to Celebrate

Most of us think about celebrating when a project is finished, a problem is completely solved, a big decision has been made, or a habit has been broken. These are certainly

303

occasions for celebrating! However, as you help your friend, learn to celebrate *throughout* the change process.

Your friend may make certain remarks which will alert you to her need for recognition, such as "It was hard, but I made it!" or "I can't believe I actually did it!" and "That is something I have been trying to do for a long time!" Be on the alert for her cues for celebration.

Don't wait for large victories, but look for small steps of progress to celebrate. Don't wait until the problem is solved or the situation is resolved. If you do, you will have missed many opportunities to express joy.

Sometimes it's difficult to find reasons to celebrate. You may have a friend who is going through a very difficult and serious problem. How can you celebrate at a time like that? If you are looking for *big* steps to celebrate, you probably will not find reasons for celebration, because most of us do not move through change quickly. However, God is always working in your friend's life, and as she obeys Him, there will be progress and reasons to celebrate!

Judy was in deep pain over the recent death of her husband. His death had been unexpected; and she felt overwhelmed, not only by her great loss, but also by all the details her husband had handled for her. But, in the midst of her grief, her friend Emily found a good reason to celebrate with her.

Judy related, "Jerry had done everything for me. When he died, I felt so inadequate. But Emily was right there. She helped me in so many ways! I'll never forget the first time I balanced the checkbook and paid all of the bills. Emily arrived at my house with a balloon that said, 'Congratulations!' and a quart of my favorite ice cream. That did more to lift me up than anything else she could have done!"

The prophet Nehemiah observed: "For the joy of the Lord is your strength and stronghold" (Nehemiah 8:10). Having her efforts recognized will bring joy to your friend and that joy will give her strength.

Finding reasons to celebrate can create happy memories that will last for years. Celebration of small steps will also balance the pain and change the content of a memory.

Evelyn had been unemployed for more than a year. The thoughtfulness of a friend had helped her through that difficult year of stress. She told me, "I had almost lost hope of ever finding a job! When I was in a state of absolute despair, my friend brought me a beautifully wrapped gift. When I opened the box, I found a pin with the letters 'Y.A.A.I.T.M.' engraved on it. As I looked at her with a puzzled expression, she exclaimed, 'I know not having a job has been very hard for you, and I've admired the way you have continued to have a good attitude despite the setbacks. You have really been an inspiration to me. That's what these letters stand for—*You Are An Inspiration To Me!* This is your medal for persevering during these past months!'"

Evelyn continued, "Soon after that, I got another job, but I will never forget how my friend's gift lifted me up and helped me turn a corner. Now when I recall that year, I don't remember the difficult times as clearly as I do my 'medal.' The whole experience has taken on a different meaning!"

Find ways to show your friend how special she is, to encourage her, and to build her up so that she can continue to persevere. Look for small steps that illustrate God's glory in her life. In doing so, you and your friend can celebrate all along the way!

The Ways of Celebration

God understands our need for celebration and reward. Ephesians 6:8 says, "Knowing that for whatever good anyone does, he will receive his reward from the Lord." Just as God recognizes our small acts of faithfulness, watch over the life of your friend and look for ways to celebrate what she *is* able to do. Even if her attempts fail, recognize her efforts. Celebrate her efforts, not just victories. You can celebrate with scrapbooks, awards, parties, gifts, or letters and cards. Ask God to show you creative ways.

Scrapbooks

After I had completed a long project, my artistic friend, Jetta, made a scrapbook for me. On the first page of the scrapbook, she drew me standing in front of a high mountain range. On my feet were enormous, heavy boots that came up to my knees. On the following pages were pictures of significant steps I had made. The last page was of me standing on level ground, having crossed each mountain peak. I had a banner in my hand that said, "Pro," and the enormous, heavy boots now fit my feet.

When she gave me the scrapbook, I was reminded of all the ways that God had, at critical points, carried me through difficulties. Although it has been many years since Jetta presented me with that scrapbook, the images she drew still come to mind when I face a large task. I am again reminded of God's faithfulness to me and of His possibilities!

You may not have a talent for drawing, but don't forget that scrapbooks can be made using snapshots, Scripture, symbols, or pictures.

Awards

Creative awards are fun to give. Use your imagination. For example, you can give your friend an Atta-Girl Award.

One woman had been sick for so long that she had lost confidence in her ability to even run errands for her family. After she had regained enough strength to go to the grocery store for the first time in several months, she returned to find an "Atta-Girl" award taped on the kitchen door. Her friend had decorated a sheet of construction paper with gold stars, and "Atta-Girl!" had been written with red glitter! Many of us would not consider a trip to the grocery store worthy of recognition, but for that woman, it was a great accomplishment! And she appreciated her friend's noticing it.

"Look for small steps that illustrate God's glory in her life. In doing so, you and your friend can celebrate all along the way!"

Parties

Parties or special events can mark steps of progress. These can range from elaborate celebrations to a visit to the frozen yogurt shop.

Two friends wanted to celebrate Betty's tenth year as a believer, so to mark the occasion, they invited her to a festive new Mexican restaurant in town. Betty told me about the evening. "Before we arrived, they arranged for special gifts to be placed at my seat. During dinner, they told me of many ways in which they had seen God work in my life, as well as the ways I had grown as a person.

"Enjoying a festive meal with my friends, opening their thoughtful gifts, and celebrating God's work in my life provided an evening I will always remember."

Whether your "party" is large or small, expensive or inexpensive, long or short, it will leave a mental impression of God's goodness and faithfulness to her.

Small Gifts

Scott was a dedicated Christian who went through an extended period of unemployment. During the time that he continually sent out resumes and interviewed for jobs without success, he took long, steady strides in his spiritual growth. When he finally got a job, a friend sent him a small trophy of a runner, with a note saying, "You ran a good race!" Scott told us he kept that small trophy by his bed for a long time, adding that few gifts had meant as much to him as that recognition of his steady progress through the struggle of unemployment.

Letters and Cards

Have you ever opened your mailbox and found a brightly colored envelope addressed to you? Can you recall the anticipation you felt as you opened it? What special message did you find inside? Did it make you feel good?

Toni told me of the encouragement she felt from the letter she received from her friend Sandi. "From time to time, I reread her words, and I experience afresh the joy I felt when I received it. She wrote, 'One day, when you stand before our glorious Lord, you will glimpse all that you've done in and through Him, by His grace. And as you cast down your crown of jewels before Him, there will be a sparkling gem for the friend you have been to me these months.'

"Sandi's letter came at a time when I really needed a word of hope and encouragement. I felt loved, appreciated, accepted, and cared about. Her words gave me the boost I needed. I felt the love of God surrounding me through her words. I will never forget her or that letter."

Balloons

What is a more festive sign of celebration than balloons? A single balloon can express great joy, especially when accompanied with a message that addresses the occasion.

Still in the hospital following heart surgery, Dianne was thrilled when her surgeon said her heart was "as good as new." When she told friends who had been praying for her, they sent her a giant, red, heart-shaped balloon with the message, "A New Heart," followed by a Scripture reference. What an exuberant and colorful way to celebrate what God had done for her!

Flowers

Historically, flowers have been a special gesture of love and appreciation.

On the day I completed and mailed the manuscript for *My Father's Child*, my husband, Wayne, brought me a dozen roses to mark the occasion. He even took snapshots of me holding the bouquet. When the pictures were printed, we posted one on our kitchen bulletin board.

That was almost three years ago, but it is still there. When I see it, I'm reminded of the exhilaration of that day, and it has encouraged me during the writing of *The Counsel of a Friend*!

Celebrate! Celebrate!

Our Father gives us many reasons to celebrate. We have a mighty God working on our behalf, and when we walk with Him, there will always be victories. We can rejoice as Paul did:

> But thanks be to God, Who in Christ always leads us in triumph [as trophies of Christ's victory] and through us spreads and makes evident the fragrance of the knowledge of God everywhere. (2 Corinthians 2:14)

Because of Him, we can celebrate! We are His trophies! He will work in us, perfecting us and bringing His work in us to completion (Philippians 1:6). So rejoice with your friend! Celebrate! Be glad and celebrate what God has done!

LIFE APPLICATIONS ⎯⎯⎯⎯⎯⎯⎯⎯

1. As a child, how did your family celebrate birthdays? Christmas? Holidays?

2. When was the last time you celebrated something?

3. What kinds of things do you and your family now celebrate? How do you celebrate these?

4. What are some things others have done for you—to encourage you, to celebrate—that have been especially meaningful?

5. What are some things you could do for your family, friends, or co-workers that would be a celebration?

6. Optional Group Exercise: Write "My name is ____
_____. I am . . ." on a blank sheet of paper,
and have someone pin it on your back. Each person
in the group then writes, on the back of everyone's
paper, positive characteristics about that person,
without signing his name. After everyone is finished
writing, remove the papers, and take turns reading
the comments. Take this time to celebrate all that
God has placed within each person! Take the paper
home and post it where you will see it daily!

SUBJECT INDEX

SCRIPTURE INDEX

317

ABOUT THE AUTHOR

Lynda D. Elliott is a social worker at the Minirth-Meier-Rice Clinic in Little Rock, Arkansas. She works with individuals, families, and leads support groups for women who are survivors of childhood abuse. Previously, Lynda trained lay counselors who worked to befriend and rehabilitate abusive parents. She was co-author of *My Father's Child: Help and Healing for Victims of Emotional, Sexual, and Physical Abuse*. She and her husband, Wayne, attend Fellowship Bible Church in Little Rock.